FUEL FOR TODAY

A 6-Month Devotional Guide For Spiritual Growth And Encouragement

RSI
PUBLISHING

Dennis L Taylor

Scriptures are taken from the New International Version of the Bible

Books may be ordered through booksellers or by contacting:
Dennis Taylor
luke252.dennis@gmail.com

RSIP
Raising the Standard International Publishing L. L. C.

ISBN: 9781955830584

Printed in the United States of America
Edition Date: April 2022

Thanks and Dedication

A few years ago, God placed in my heart a burden to write out my devotions. As time passed several people encouraged me to get them published. I laughed and I never thought anything else about it. You're talking about a guy who barely passed high school English, much less write a book. That was like God asking Noah to build an ark. Well, here it is. I heard what God said, and I gave my best.

I want to dedicate this devotional book to my parents, Linda and Kenneth Taylor. My parents not only told me about Jesus, but they also showed me Jesus. They raised me in a loving Christian home and showed me how to walk out my Christian faith. At an early age, my parents led our family in family devotions right before bedtime. We would sing little choruses like "Jesus Loves Me" or "Deep and Wide". Then our dad would share a couple of scriptures, and we would all talk about them. Then we would simply pray, and then we would "climb the tree". In other words, my brother, sister, and I would get on the bed, and jump on our dad as he was standing there with his muscles flexed. After all that, we would climb our way to his shoulders and crow like roosters. I never knew how this simple act would change my life forever. "Thank you, Lord, for blessing me with parents who cared for me, prayed over me, and taught me all about your love."

I also want to thank my sister, Sherry Turoski, for doing the first series of editing of this book. Never once did she laugh at me - at least to my face. She took time out of her busy schedule to read through every devotion and covered it all in prayer. She is a loving mom, school teacher, a disciple of Christ, and one of the godliest people I know. She has always been one of the biggest encouragements, and she has always had my back, no matter what. Thanks again and just know how much I appreciate everything you do for me.

Thank you, Wanda Rodgers, Jeannette Ahmie, Sonia Banks, Rebekah Young, Renee Magnuson, and Debbie Lord. They spent many hours doing the final editing, but they also prayed over every sentence and every word. You all are a huge blessing to me. Thank you for your time and patience with me. You all are so gracious and kind. May God bless you and keep you.

Roy Anderson, you did an amazing job on the cover of this book. I gave you a thought and you made it come alive. I know I joke with you about this, but it is so true. I say I will buy my own book just to have a picture of the cover. Thank you so much for your willingness to help a brother out. You are a blessing and tool that God is using to change this world. I love you, and I pray God's greatest blessing on you today. Keep on keeping on.

Last but not least, I want to thank Kim Goodson for inspiring me to write my thoughts down on paper. Thanks for your encouragement, wisdom, and your friendship. I could never have done this without you. May God bless you and your beautiful family.

Foreword

I'm sort of a devotional junkie. My bookshelves at both my church office and my home office are filled with hundreds of devotionals that I have read as part of my daily prayer life or what I like to call my "TAWG – time alone with God" for over 40 years. I believe it is the one thing we must do to develop intimacy with Christ, as well as the greatest privilege and joy. I especially like devotionals that are short readings for the day, filled with scripture and that provide a challenge or step of action. "Fuel for the Day", this excellent book by Dennis Taylor that you hold in your hands is one of those devotionals. It is filled with "pure spiritual milk" that we are called to crave according to 1 Peter 2:2, along with a simplicity of the gospel that challenges us to authentic faith and pure devotion to Christ!

I know the devotions in "Fuel for the Day" are authentic because I personally have known the author since he was a junior high student in my Youth Ministry. I also get to continue to see him living out his faith up-close as he is married to my sister, (the Former Laura Durham) and we have had the privilege of serving together in ministry over several years. Dennis Taylor writes from his heart, his experience and most of all from a deep well of relationship with Jesus. It's transformational truth that will encourage you, challenge you and "spur you on towards love and good deeds" (Hebrews 10:24). This is a wonderful tool to help you daily get your fuel and stay on fire for God!

Billy Durham
Director of Prayer and Leadership Development
Park Ave. Baptist Church – Titusville, Florida

Sandpaper

Don't you love it when God shows you a weakness about yourself? We are all just a work in progress. I pictured Jesus this morning taking me to His workshop and making some fine adjustments. He sanded me down just a hair with His gentle hand. I could see that sparkle of love in His eyes and sensed the compassion in His heart. I received what He said to me this morning, but it's not always easy to hear a word of correction. In Ephesians 1:15-19, Paul prayed a specific prayer over his friends and his brothers and sisters in Christ. He wasn't focused on himself. He was thinking of those around him, and he cared enough to pray for them.

Look at his prayer. Sense the love in his heart for his friends. Ephesians 1:15-19: "For this reason, ever since I heard about your faith in the Lord Jesus and your love for all the saints, I have not stopped giving thanks for you, remembering you in my prayers. I keep asking that the God of our Lord Jesus Christ, the glorious Father, may give you the Spirit of wisdom and revelation, so that you know him better. I pray also that the eyes of your heart may be enlightened in order that you may know the hope to which he has called you, the riches of his glorious inheritance in the saints, and his incomparably great power for us who believe."

Do you dare pray this over your friends today?

I can study God's Word for hours and not get enough, but I find it hard to sit over ten minutes talking with the Lord. In His workshop, He revealed to me that I don't pray enough for the Church and my friends. Yes, I have a plan in place; I know what I need to do. Now I must implement the plan. "Lord, help me to be a praying Paul. Help me to take my eyes off myself and open my spiritual eyes. Help me to be creative in my prayer time with you, and let it be a top priority. Thank you, Lord, for not using the really coarse sandpaper."

Challenge for today: Reread the verses above and lean into Him to figure out your prayer plan.

A Prayer for The Church

Paul prays a beautiful and powerful prayer over two local churches of his day. I want to share this prayer with you, but I also want to challenge you to pray this over your local body of believers. The challenge is to pray this prayer for seven days straight, and then ask God, "What would you have me to do now?" Are you in?

In Philippians 1:9-11 Paul prays, "And this is my prayer: that your love may abound more and more in knowledge and depth of insight, so that you may be able to discern what is best and may be pure and blameless until the day of Christ, filled with the fruit of righteousness that comes through Jesus Christ to the glory and praise of God." Amen.

The Church is under constant attack, and Satan never gives up. He uses everything in his arsenal to make us stumble along the way. He will use jealousy, pride, lies, and deceit to destroy us. More than ever before, we need to get down on our knees and pray for wisdom, discernment, and the power of the Holy Spirit to fill our lives. Take time to feast on God's Word and invest time alone with your Heavenly Father. Then experience the transformation that God wants to bring to your life and to His Church. Grow in His love. As we grow in His love, He will bless us with knowledge, wisdom, and discernment. He will give us everything we need as believers to grow His Church and overcome the schemes of Satan. Make an investment today and set aside time to pray for the Church of Jesus Christ. We will be amazed how God takes a small investment and triples our return. Invest in prayer for His Church and watch how God will change the hearts of people.

Challenge for today: Make a difference, pray over the Church. Let's encourage one another and grow in love. Let us walk in humility, wisdom, and compassion. Pursue holiness and guard your mind against the evil one. Keep the faith and fight the good fight. Let's kick some dents in the gates of hell.

A Needed Word

Ezekiel 18:30-32: "Therefore, O house of Israel, I will judge you, each one according to his ways, declares the Sovereign Lord. Repent! Turn away from all your offenses; then sin will not be your downfall. Rid yourself of all the offenses you have committed and get a new heart and a new spirit. Why will you die? O, house of Israel? For I take no pleasure in the death of anyone, declares the Sovereign Lord. Repent and live!"

Such a needed word for us today. Repent means to turn a complete 180 degrees and walk in a new direction. What do you need to give to the Lord? Is it that hidden sin that has been haunting you for years? Is it eating away little by little?

Lamentations 3:40-42: "Let us examine our ways and test them and let us return to the Lord. Let us lift up our hearts and our hands to God in heaven, and say: We have sinned and rebelled and you have not forgiven."

It's time to walk away from that old way of living and walk in the newness of Christ. Repent and lay it at the feet of Jesus. He is faithful and just, and He will forgive you. Are you ready to dump that heavy load? Are you ready to experience true peace in your life? Repent and really live. It is time to come clean and let go of the baggage and the garbage of life that is weighing you down. Experience the freedom found only in a personal relationship with Jesus Christ.

Challenge for today: Pray Psalm 51:1-12, and let all pretense go. Call out to the Lord. Be renewed and refreshed. I pray for you courage, strength, and joy. Know this: God is still in the restoration business. Give thanks to the Lord and praise Him for His goodness.

What Do You Want Jesus to Do for You?

Matthew 20:29-34: "As Jesus and his disciples were leaving Jericho, a large crowd followed him. Two blind men were sitting by the roadside, and when they heard that Jesus was going by, they shouted, 'Lord, Son of David, have mercy on us!' The crowd rebuked them and told them to be quiet, but they shouted all the louder, 'Lord, Son of David, have mercy on us!' Jesus stopped and called them, 'What do you want me to do for you?' he asked. 'Lord,' they answered, 'We want our sight.' Jesus had compassion on them and touched their eyes. Immediately they received their sight and followed him."

Wow. What a question. What if Jesus were to ask you that very same question: What do you want me to do for you? How would you answer that question? The sad thing is, most of us have no idea what we want God to do for us, or in us. What are your desires, hopes, dreams, and passions? What has God placed in your heart? Psalm 37:4: "Delight yourself in the Lord and he will give you the desires of your heart."

I encourage you to dive deep into your relationship with your Heavenly Father and begin to have some hard conversations with the Lord. Stop pushing Him away. Throw it all out there and talk with God openly about your heart's desires. It's time to live out what God has placed in you. Don't allow fear to rule your life and kill your dreams. Stop living from day to day, just existing. Live out the dreams God has put in your heart.

How would you answer the question today? "Lord, do a work in my friend's life, help them to follow hard after you, and give them the guts to do what you have called them to do. Amen."

Challenge for today: Define your passion and seek the Lord with all your heart. Then you will be able to answer His question.

What Are You Focused On?

We have missed out on so many things since the Corona virus hit. My beloved father-in-law's big celebration after he passed away, my niece's wedding, church services, and March Madness. When I say March Madness, many of you know exactly what I am talking about. It is college basketball's road to the National Championship. The top college basketball teams come together to decide who is the number one college team in the country. Yes, there are blowouts and huge wins. There are very close games and huge upsets every year. Small schools compete against huge schools. This is big time college basketball at its finest.

Many of the games come down to that last shot or that final free throw. Put yourself in their shoes for a moment. Millions of people are watching on TV, and thousands of people are in the stands. Everybody is on their feet yelling and screaming and looking straight at you. Fans are waving their hands, jumping up and down, and doing everything possible to distract you. Where is your focus? What are you looking at while you are about to take the biggest shot of your life? Are you looking at the crowd or all the craziness going on around you? No, you are focused on the rim. You are seeing your shot going in. You are so focused on that rim that you don't even see the crowd, much less hear them. You hit the shot, and your team wins the game. A storybook ending.

I encourage you to read Psalm 16. This Psalm is written by David, the little boy who killed Goliath with a slingshot and a rock. Psalm 16:8: "I have set the Lord always before me, because he is at my right hand, I will not be shaken."

Talk about the pressure of missing a shot. What about David? Forget March Madness. What would have happened if David had missed that shot? But David stood firm, and he didn't miss. You see, David's focus wasn't on the crowd or the giant. David's focus was on someone bigger than Goliath. That is why David was not afraid of him. The giant was bigger than David, but God was bigger than the giant. David was focused on the Lord.

Challenge for today: I don't know what you are facing today or what you are going through. But I do know this, my God is bigger than any problem you are facing. Take your eyes off the giants that you are facing and turn them to the One who can overcome them. Set the Lord before you and turn your focus to Him. You will not be shaken.

Will The Real Lion Please Stand Up?

irst Peter 5:6-9: "Humble yourselves, therefore, under God's mighty hand, that he may lift you up in due time. Cast all your anxiety on him because he cares for you. Be self-controlled and alert. Your enemy the devil prowls around like a roaring lion looking for someone to devour. Resist him, standing firm in the faith, because you know that your brothers throughout the world are undergoing the same kind of suffering."

There are four things that jump off the page to me.
1. Be humble.
2. Stop worrying.
3. Be self-controlled and spiritually alert.
4. Stand firm in your faith.

As Christians, we are under constant attack from the enemy, and he never gives up. He knows his time is short, and he is fighting a losing battle. His selfish pride will not allow him to quit. The one thing I want you to see is that the devil is not a roaring lion. He is an imposter. God's Word tells us here that he prowls around like a roaring lion. It doesn't necessarily say he is a roaring lion. He is a want-to-be. The devil wants us to think that he is in control. He wants us to feel hopeless and helpless. Think about it, he is the one who is defeated, and his days are numbered. He is like that snake that had his head severed. He is dead, but he is still wiggling around causing as much fear as he can before he must go. Jesus is the Lion of Judah. He is the one and only True King. His voice alone shatters the enemy. He rules and reigns and is worthy of all praise and glory.

Listen to this encouraging word found in First Peter 5:10-11, "And the God of all grace, who called you to his eternal glory in Christ, after you have suffered a little while, will himself restore you and make you strong, firm and steadfast. To him be the power for ever and ever. Amen."

Challenge for today: Hold on to this truth and share it with a friend. God is good, and He is good all the time. He wants to restore you and make you strong, firm, and steadfast.

Who Will You Serve?

Have you ever had that relative who is straightforward in what they say? You know, the one that says what's on his or her mind, and there is no second guessing where they stand on any issue. I have learned to really appreciate those kinds of people. They are real, and there is no pretense about them. What you see is what you get, and you know where you stand with them.

I want to share a straightforward word with you from Deuteronomy 30:15-18: "See, I set before you today life and prosperity, death and destruction. For I command you today to love the Lord your God, to walk in His ways, and keep His commands, decrees and laws; then you will live and increase, and the Lord your God will bless you in the land you are entering to possess. But if your heart turns away and you are not obedient, and if you are drawn away to bow down to other gods and worship them. I declare to you this day that you will certainly be destroyed."

Does it get any plainer than that? I believe this is a message this great nation needs to hear without apology. We live in a country founded on Christian principles by godly men and women. God has blessed this country because of our obedience to Him, but we have turned our backs on Almighty God. We are running after all the wrong things. We worship and serve other gods and our own selfish ways. This is a wakeup call to the world. Are we going to listen?

Deuteronomy 30:19-20 continues on, "This day I call heaven and earth as witnesses against you that I have set before you life and death, blessings and curses. Now choose life, so that you and your children may live and that you may love the Lord your God, listen to his voice, and hold fast to Him."

Who will you serve? Choose well. Joshua says it best in Joshua 24:14-15: "Now fear the Lord and serve him with faithfulness. Throw away the gods your forefathers worshiped beyond the river and in Egypt and serve the Lord. But if serving the Lord seems undesirable to you, then choose for yourselves this day whom you will serve, whether the gods your forefathers served beyond the river, or the gods of the Amorites, in whose land you are living. But as for me and my household, we will serve the Lord."

There is no beating around the bush. It's a straightforward, in your face, word from God. Choose well.

Challenge for today: Set aside ten extra minutes and take time to focus only on your Father's voice. Then ask yourself, who do I serve? Does God have first place in my heart? Don't move until He shows you the answers.

Building Memories

How many times have you spent a lot of money on a present for your little child or grandchild, and you wrapped it up in a big box? When the time came to unwrap the present, they tore into the box and pulled out the present you bought for them. They acknowledged the present, and of course they said, "Thank you." But for the next two hours, all they played with was the huge empty box. You could have saved a lot of money and not bought the expensive present.

Some of my fondest memories of my grandparents weren't about big expensive gifts or trips. They were simple things and didn't cost much of anything. I remember going to my grandparents' house, climbing the fig trees, and having a fig war. I remember spending hours raking up leaves in the yard, then destroying the piles by running through them, and diving into the pile. I remember our snack times like it was yesterday. There was a steady flow of sweet tea, cookies, and pound cakes. Why did it seem like we never could finish our games before we had to leave?

I could talk about my childhood memories with my parents all day long, but this devotion couldn't hold it all. What sticks out most to me is that they gave us the gift of their presence. They were always there. Yes, they gave us some amazing gifts; my all-time favorite was the Silver Streak go-kart. We had fun with that thing, until my brother ran me down with it. I probably deserved it. But what I remember the most was doing things that didn't cost money. I remember throwing the ball with my dad on the mound he built in the backyard while my mom sat out in the lawn chair and watched. I remember building a tent in the living room and watching TV while eating sandwiches and popcorn. I remember our nighttime devotions, and swimming in our above ground pool all day long. I will never forget those days and the feeling of being so loved.

Challenge for today: Build memories with those you love. It doesn't have to cost a lot of money, and you don't have to travel around the world to do it. Build a tent in the living room and watch a whole movie together. Take a long walk, and don't worry about how long it takes you to get back. Learn to celebrate the little things and be thankful for the small blessings in life. Those are the ones that will mean the most to you down the road anyway. "Thank you, Lord, for the blessings of life. To You be all the glory and praise."

Worship

Psalm 95:6-7: "Come, let us bow down in worship, let us kneel before the Lord our Maker; for He is our God, and we are the people of his pasture, the flock under his care."

Worship is collective, vocal, vibrant, God-centered, and focused on truth. Authentic worship renews your strength. Authentic worship reconnects you with God, and authentic worship restores your perspective. Authentic worship rekindles your hope. Authentic worship rebuilds your confidence, and authentic worship restores your joy. Authentic worship releases your anxieties. Worship refocuses your eyes on God. Worship gets our attention off ourselves. It is an outpouring of our hearts.

Psalm 96:1-4: "Sing to the Lord a new song; sing to the Lord, all the earth. Sing to the Lord, praise His name; proclaim His salvation day after day. Declare His glory among the nations, His marvelous deeds among all peoples. For great is the Lord and most worthy of praise; He is to be feared among all gods."

Why would one not set aside time to worship? Let's worship Him today. Let's give Him the glory He deserves. Let's celebrate our King. Let's break out in song and thanksgiving. Praise His holy name and worship Him alone.

The first time I sang choruses at youth camp was the first time I truly began to worship in song. Music can open our hearts for His movement and teaching in our lives. The way we worship can be with singing, playing instruments, and even dancing with hands lifted high. It can also be so much more. Every movement, thought, and response can be our worship.

Challenge for today: Take time to identify what is grabbing your attention. What are you focused on and what consumes your time? Then, be willing to rearrange your priorities and place God at the front of the line. Give Him first place and worship Him with passion. He alone is worthy of our praise.

Use Your Gift

I want to share a funny little story I read out of a book two years ago. This story is about a woman shouting at her son who was hiding under the bed on a Sunday morning. He was crying and refusing to go to their church that had been having some problems. "Come out this minute," the woman shouted. "You're ruining your suit!" "I don't care about my suit," the son said. "You have to go to church!" "Tell me one good reason," the son said. "I will tell you three! People are depending on you, it honors God, and you are the pastor."

I hope that is not your pastor. Romans 13:6-8: "We have different gifts, according to the grace given us. If a man's gift is prophesying, let him use it in proportion to his faith. If it is serving, let him serve; if it is teaching, let him teach; if it is encouraging, let him encourage; if it is contributing to the needs of others, let him give generously; if it is leading, let him govern diligently; if it is showing mercy, let him do it cheerfully."

What is your gift? What desires and passions has God placed in you? I encourage you to discover your gift that God has given you. Develop it and share it with the world. I truly believe that the most miserable person on the face of the planet is the person who is gifted by God but doesn't use his gift. My youth pastor once said, "Use it or lose it." God wants to use the gift He has placed inside of you. What is holding you back?

Challenge for today: I encourage you to take a spiritual gift test online. They are easy to find on the internet, and it will only take a few minutes to fill out. Check out your results and see if you are already involved in your gifting. Ask close friends what they think is your spiritual gift and talent. Then use your gifts and encourage others because it honors God.

Ball And Chain

As Christians, we know we have received forgiveness, but we don't fully understand the depth of God's mercy. When we don't embrace the forgiveness that He so freely gives us, we begin to sink into a life of just existing. Think about it. Our past sins and mess-ups are like a huge ball and chain. We try to pretend it's not there; then we try our best to live with it. Eventually it will wear us down and lead us to a life of worry, anxiety, depression, and guilt.

There is good news. We don't have to carry that ball and chain around with us. When we finally decide to take our sins, guilt, and worries to the Lord, He takes them and casts them into His ocean of forgiveness. Until we experience the fullness of God's grace, we will never be able to fully forgive others. We can't give what we haven't received. King David wrote Psalm 32:5 to the Lord, "Then I acknowledged my sin to you and did not cover up my iniquity. I said, 'I will confess my transgressions to the Lord'-and you forgave the guilt of my sin."

When we reveal our hearts to God, healing starts. Release the bitterness, guilt, and the heartaches. Then receive God's amazing grace. Now it's time to forgive those who have hurt you. Get rid of that ball and chain and experience freedom found only in a relationship with Jesus Christ.

Challenge for today: Grab a sheet of paper and a pencil. Then simply ask God to whom you need to go to and make things right? Is there unforgiveness, hatred, envy, or even bitterness in any relationship in your life? Write those names down and ask God to give you an open door to make things right with each person. It is time to dump all that worry, stress, and unforgiveness. Break free from that ball and chain.

Give Him What He Deserves

Have you ever wondered where it all went wrong with Satan? He had it made. He had a great position, but it was not enough. Satan was after God's glory. He refused to honor the Lord and now targets anybody he can deceive to strike at the heart of God. He is not just out to destroy you; he is out to tarnish God's glory. We are children of God; we are His pride and joy. If Satan can gash our hearts, he can break the heart of God.

It is so hard to express what I am feeling deep in my soul, but there is nothing better than a relationship with Jesus. To be loved by the King of the universe is second to none. He has withheld nothing from us, and He gave us His very best. John 10:10: "The thief comes only to steal and kill and destroy; I have come that they may have life and have it to the full."

Don't give Satan an inch in your life. Don't even crack the door to his lies and tactics because he will try to slither in. Yes, the battle has been won, but we are still in a fight. Life is short. God is all powerful. Don't shrink back. Finish strong and live for the glory of the Lord. Know this, God doesn't exist for your glory, but we exist for His glory. I encourage you to give God what He deserves, which is glory. Psalm 66:1-2: "Shout with joy to God, all the earth. Sing the glory of his name; make his praise glorious!"

Live for the glory of the Lord. Let's be found faithful.

Challenge for today: Take time to recognize God's goodness throughout the day. Thank Him for three things in your life that have been a blessing to you. If one of those things happens to be a special person, send a written note or text to let them know how thankful you are. As always, He deserves all the praise.

Knock The Dust Off

If I had my choice, I would wear T-shirts and jeans every day of the week. I hate to admit it, but there are only seven shirts that I wear on a regular basis. Last week I started going through my closet and wondering why everything was crammed together. To my surprise, I counted at least 20 shirts. Some shirts have been in my closet for more than 20 years. Some of those shirts were nice, and I began to wonder why I never wore them. They have been hanging in my closet so long that they have gathered a ton of dust, especially around the shoulders. Wow, I could have been wearing these shirts all this time. I just had to knock the dust off them. Talk about regrets.

What do you need to knock the dust off at your house today, besides the end tables? I don't know about you, but I will have to knock the dust off my Sunday shoes. This past year has been one of the craziest years of my life, to say the least. Because of the Covid Virus, life as we know it has been turned upside down. The one thing I missed the most was going to church and worshiping with friends and family. There is an old saying that goes something like this, "Absence makes the heart grow fonder." How many times do we take friends and family for granted? How about gathering on Sunday to worship our Lord Jesus Christ face to face. Praising God, joking with friends, and just enjoying God together. With churches slowly getting back in the flow of meeting together again, I think many of us will appreciate each other a bit more. I know all the pastors and teachers love having everyone back. If they are like me, you get tired of sharing in front of a lifeless camera on Facebook Live. Don't get me wrong, during these difficult times, it was so nice to have Facebook Live and Zoom, but it's not the same.

I encourage believers who have fallen out of touch with their local body of believers. Talk about some dusty church shoes. Come on, wipe them off, wax them up, and buff them out. Or come just as they are. Get back in fellowship with family. We all need the encouragement of God's Word and other believers. Hebrews 10:24-25: "And let us consider how we may spur one another on towards love and good deeds. Let us not give up meeting together, as some are in the habit of doing, but let us encourage- and all the more as you see the Day approaching."

Challenge for today: Let's get back at it and get connected to your local body of believers. It's time to jump back in and use your gifts for His glory. Don't just attend church. Find a small group where you can connect with people your age. Then encourage others to do the same.

Do You Need Help Today?

There are things in life that will knock you to your knees and make you realize what is important in life. The death of a loved one is never easy. It is so hard to let go and even harder to understand. How about the loss of a job, a fair-weather friend, surgery, or just bad health? Where do you find the strength and the courage to face these things? God has never promised us an easy life. He has never given us a free pass from heartache, troubles, or stress. He has promised us the assuring presence of the Holy Spirit. The Holy Spirit serves as a rudder for the ship of our soul. He keeps us afloat and on track. The Christian life is not a solo journey.

Ephesians 1:13-14: "And you also were included in Christ when you heard the word of truth, the gospel of salvation. Having believed you were marked in him with a seal, the promised Holy Spirit, who is a deposit guaranteeing our inheritance until the redemption of those who are God's possession-to the praise of his glory."

When we accept Christ, God seals us with the Holy Spirit. God paid too high of a price for us to leave us unguarded. God's Spirit confirms that we belong to Him. God's Spirit whispers, "You are mine. I bought you. I sealed you and no one can take you from Me."

Romans 5:5: "Hope does not disappoint us, because God has poured out His love into our hearts by the Holy Spirit, whom he has given us."

The Holy Spirit pours God's love into our hearts, not the love for God, but the love of God. Picture the Father handing a bucket of His pure love to the Holy Spirit and instructing Him, "Pour this over their hearts."

Romans 8:26-27: "In the same way, the Spirit helps us in our weakness. We do not know what we ought to pray for, but the Spirit himself intercedes for us with groans and words cannot express. And he who searches our hearts knows the mind of the Spirit, because the Spirit intercedes for the saints in accordance with God's will."

The Spirit comes to the aid of our weakness and hurt. The Spirit Himself is pleading for us and interceding for us. None of us pray enough, but we all pray more than we think. The Holy Spirit turns our sighs into petitions. Yes, He speaks for you, even when you don't know what to pray. God is on your side; put your hope in Him. If you are in Christ, you have been marked. You have been sealed, and He is interceding for you. You may be facing a Goliath, but you don't have to face him alone. Christ in you, the Hope of all glory, lives inside of you - Colossians 1:27.

Challenge for today: Make a list of things in life that cause you stress and anxiety. I encourage you to share that list with a close friend. Talk it over with your Heavenly Father and hand it all over to Him and trust Him with it all. Cast all your care on Him for He cares for you. You can trust Him with them.

Random Question

I want to get you thinking. So, I will start this off with a question or two. What was the last thing you did as the Church of Jesus Christ that required God's power to be accomplished? How long has it been?

There are so many struggling churches because we have developed a watered-down version of the Christian faith that looks nothing like the vibrant, life-changing, world-impacting, risk-taking faith of the early church. I am not being negative, but I am just writing down thoughts that are running through my mind. When I read about the early church, they were not afraid to take risks. They gave sacrificially, and they were not scared to share their faith. They were not hesitant to try new things.

Look at the early Church in Acts 2:42-47, "They devoted themselves to the apostles' teachings and to the fellowship, to the breaking of bread and to prayer. Everyone was filled with awe, and many wonders and miraculous signs were done by the apostles. All the believers were together and had everything in common. Selling their possessions and goods, they gave to anyone who had need. Every day they continued to meet together in the temple courts. They broke bread in their homes and ate together with glad and sincere hearts, praising God and enjoying the favor of all people. And the Lord added to their number daily those who were saved."

The early Church was devoted to the Word of God, and they were willing to lay down their lives for each other. They didn't hesitate to make sacrifices for those who were in need around them. They were willing to do anything to help the Body of Believers. That is why God added to their number daily. Why are we so hesitant?

I keep going back to the same question that is so hard for me to answer. What was the last thing I did as the Church of Jesus Christ that required God's power to be accomplished? To walk on water, we first must get out of the boat. What has God placed in your heart, but you have always been too scared to go after? What is holding you back from going all in with God?

Challenge for today: Give this question some thought, sit down, and talk with God about it. Try to do more listening than talking. I dare you to sit and listen to Him for five minutes. Take time to reflect on your life, but also ask God for the willingness to do whatever He has called you to do.

A Work in Progress

When Jesus chose the Twelve, He didn't choose a single rabbi or scribe. He certainly didn't choose a Pharisee or Sadducee. He didn't even choose a priest. Not one of the men He chose came from the religious establishment. He chose men who were not theologically trained. He chose fishermen, tax collectors, and other hard-working men. He used these men to turn the world upside down. (Acts 17:6) It wasn't because they had extraordinary talents, incredible intellectual abilities, or powerful political influence. They turned the world upside down because God worked through them to do it. He looks for availability, not ability.

First Corinthians 1:27-28: "But God has chosen the foolish things of the world to put to shame the wise, and God has chosen the weak things of this world to put to shame the things that are mighty."

God loves to use ordinary people to do extraordinary things, so that no man can boast before Him. These men abandoned their nets, left their fields, and left their tax tables behind. They laid aside everything they ever knew, to be trained for something for which they had no natural aptitude. Jesus gave them ministry opportunities, instructed them, encouraged them, and patiently taught them. But they were hardheaded like you and I.

These twelve disciples struggled when it came to the learning process.
1. They lacked spiritual understanding. They were slow to hear and slow to understand. Even after the resurrection, Jesus spent an additional 40 days here on earth teaching them.
2. They lacked humility. They were self-absorbed, self-centered, and proud. They spent so much time arguing over who was the greatest. (Matthew 20:20-28)
3. They lacked faith. Four times alone, Jesus says to them, "O you of little faith."
4. They lacked commitment. While the crowds were cheering and miracles were being performed, they were all on board. But as soon as the soldiers came to take Jesus in the Garden, they all scattered.
5. They lacked power. The funny thing is the twelve sound a lot like us. We still look at that group and wonder why Jesus didn't just start all over and pick a whole different team. Second Corinthians 12:9: "His strength is made perfect in weakness."

Acts 4:13 says, "Now when they saw the boldness of Peter and John, and perceived that they were uneducated and untrained men, they marveled. And they realized that they had been with Jesus."

Challenge for today: Can the same be said of us? Know this: we are all a work in progress. You are not going to be perfect, but keep leaning in on Christ and trust His work in you. If Christ could use those twelve to turn the world upside down, He can truly use us. Dream big because we serve a Big God.

Replace Fear with Faith

One of the greatest examples in God's Word of how to replace fear with faith comes from First Samuel 17. We all know the story of David and Goliath. As a young boy, I remember sitting on the edge of the bed imagining what it would be like to be in David's shoes. David expected victory, but most everybody else thought Goliath was too big to defeat. David thought he was too big to miss.

Saul and his entire army were paralyzed and found themselves in a difficult place. They were fearful because they followed four destructive steps.
1. Focused only on the problem. (First Samuel 17:4-10)
2. Expected to be defeated. (First Samuel 17:11)
3. Attitude of self-protection. (First Samuel 17:23-24)
4. Ran from the problem. (First Samuel 17:24)

Because of these four flaws, they stalled out in life and were going nowhere fast.

David gives us a different perspective. He was in the same situation as Saul, but he made five positive choices to live in victory.
1. He focused on God. (First Samuel 17:26)
2. Anticipated God's help. (First Samuel 17:45-47)
3. He insisted on being involved. (First Samuel 17:28-32)
4. He took time to prepare. (First Samuel 17:38-40)
5. He had an impact on everybody around him. (First Samuel 17:51-52)

Are you living in fear or faith today? It's a choice we must choose every day. Whatever you are going through, God is bigger. Whatever your weakness is, God is stronger.

Challenge for today: Raise your expectations of what God can do. Replace fear with faith. "Thank you, Lord." Let's live a life of faith and know that He is with us. We have His promise that He will never leave us or forsake us. Let's walk in victory with an attitude of faith.

He Answered the Knock

In Matthew 19:14 Jesus said, "Let the little children come to me, and do not hinder them, for the kingdom of heaven belongs to such as these."

I was five years old when I opened my heart's door to Jesus. I remember it like it was yesterday. My mom and dad played a huge role in that, and I am forever grateful. What a blessing to have parents who nurtured me in the ways of God. My mind also goes back to a lady named Mrs. Moody. She taught me in Sunday School, and I saw Jesus in her. I remember her being so kind and friendly. I can still see her teaching us and loving us as we walked out of her class. Mrs. Moody impacted my life. She wasn't famous or some big-time minister, and she never wrote a book, but she helped change my life forever.

I had the greatest opportunity to pray with an eight-year-old boy named Hays. His parents invited me to sit on the back porch to help him receive Jesus Christ into his heart. What a blessing to be a part of leading him to the Lord. I looked into Hays' eyes, and I saw excitement, wonder, pure joy, and peace. His face lit up like a Christmas tree and a huge smile covered his face. That is what it's all about. It is so hard to put all of this in a short devotion, but I left their house on cloud nine. I got in the car and pumped up the praise, and I celebrated. Who were the "Mrs. Moody's" in your life? Are you being a "Mrs. Moody" for someone?

So many times, we feel insignificant, and at times we wonder if we are making a difference. Some have taught Sunday School, discipled students, and invested in children for years and years. Know this: you are making a huge investment, and it will be worth your time. Keep reflecting Christ's love in the hearts of the children and students around you.

Challenge for today: Take every opportunity to pour Jesus over everyone you meet. You are changing this world one life at a time. Keep it going, and don't grow tired of fulfilling your calling.

Make Your Father Proud

We all have our weaknesses, and we all have sin in our lives. It blows us away to know that God knows our heart, and He sees everything that goes on in our mind. Yes, we may hide it even from the people who know us the best, but God sees it all. I encourage you to guard your heart, push aside your old life, and yield everything to your Heavenly Father.

Romans 6:11-14: "Count yourselves dead to sin but alive to God in Christ Jesus. Therefore, do not let sin reign in your mortal body so that you obey its evil desires. Do not offer the parts of your body to sin, as instruments of wickedness, but rather offer yourselves to God, as those who have been brought from death to life; and offer the parts of your body to him as an instrument of righteousness. For sin shall not be your master, because you are not under the law, but under grace."

Offer your entire life as an instrument of righteousness to the Lord. You are dead to sin and alive in Him. Celebrate that today.

Let's grab some more truth to chew on. First Corinthians 6:18-20: "Flee from sexual immorality. All other sins a man commits are outside his body, but he who sins sexually sins against his own body. Do you not know that your body is the temple of the Holy Spirit, who is in you, whom you have received from God? You are not your own; you were bought with a price. Therefore, honor God with your body."

Make your Father proud of how you live your life. God has called us to live a life of holiness. It's not optional. What do you need to hand over to Jesus Christ today? Is there a secret sin that nobody knows about? Is there someone you need to forgive, or is there someone you need to call and say, "I am sorry, can you forgive me?" Don't push it off and wait for another day. Honor God today.

Challenge for today: Read First John 1:9: "If we confess our sins, he is faithful and just and will forgive us our sins and purify us from all unrighteousness."

Take this opportunity to have a time of confession. That means we need to sit in His presence and come clean with our Heavenly Father. It's time to be real and drop the pretense. What do you need to get off your chest? Know that He is faithful and just and

He is willing to forgive. Drop that heavy load that you have been carrying. He cares for you.

A Prayer of Blessings

Numbers 6:22-26: "The Lord said to Moses, 'Tell Aaron and his sons, 'This is how you are to bless the Israelites.' Say to them: 'The Lord bless you and keep you; the Lord makes his face shine upon you and be gracious to you; the Lord turns his face toward you and gives you peace.'"

God is good, and He is good all the time. Have you ever noticed that some of the greatest blessings of life come in small packages? Bigger doesn't necessarily mean better. Just ask that young lady who received a ring from a young man who knelt in front of her with a little box. It changed her life forever. Yes, it was a small token of love, but it's something bigger than what the human eye can see. That young man just made a huge commitment to that young lady and said to her, "I will love you forever." When we pray a blessing over someone, it may not seem like a big deal, but it is much more than the human eye can understand. Sometimes we want to do some huge thing for God. We want to speak to the thousands, or we may want to write a book. God loves the little gifts that we give to people daily. Pray prayers of blessings over someone today. When we pray these prayers of blessings, we are giving them gifts that will change their lives.

"God bless you and keep you; let his face shine on you and be gracious to you; and give you peace." That felt good.

Challenge for today: This is a prayer of blessing, and I encourage you to pray this simple prayer over three people today. Then continue to pray this same prayer over them consistently for seven days. Write down what God shows you and what He does in their lives.

He Has Risen

Matthew 28:1-6: "After the Sabbath, at dawn on the first day of the week, Mary Magdalene and the other Mary went to look at the tomb. There was a violent earthquake, and an angel of the Lord came down from heaven and, going to the tomb, rolled back the stone and sat on it. His appearance was like lightning, and his clothes were white as snow. The guards were so afraid of him that they shook and became like dead men. The angel said to the women, 'Do not be afraid, for I know that you are looking for Jesus, who was crucified. He is not here; he has risen, just as he said. Come and see the place where he lay.'"

Yes, our Jesus was flogged and nearly beaten to death. He was stripped and humiliated in front of everybody. They placed a crown of thorns on His head and spit on Him. He was nailed to a cross like a common thief. He suffered, bled, and died. He could have called 10,000 angels down to pull him off that cross, but he chose to take our punishment. He chose to hang on that cross for you and me. He took our place. Joseph of Arimathea came and prepared Jesus' body and placed him in a tomb. What a tragic way to die, but it is a good thing the story doesn't stop there. We get to celebrate on Easter because of what Christ did for us so many years ago. The tomb could not hold Him in the grave; sin had no power over Him. *He has risen!* He is alive and well, and He is sitting at the right hand of the Father. He is the giver of life. He is the Lord of Lords and the King of Kings. He is my personal Lord and Savior. Satan and death have been defeated because of His great love for us. There is victory in Jesus Christ. If you are in Christ, you are on the winning team and loved by the very Creator of heaven and earth.

Challenge for today: Praise Him today. Yes, let's celebrate what Christ has done for us, but tomorrow we have a job to do. We are called to go and tell. Go and make disciples of all nations, baptizing them in the name of the Father and of the Son and of the Holy Spirit. He has Risen! Celebrate, and then get busy.

Four Things You Must Know

There are four things that you need to know before you leave this earth. It has nothing to do with reading, writing, or arithmetic. It has everything to do with Jesus. How do you receive Christ? Or some may ask it this way: How do I become born again? This is the message we need to share with the world.

First, we must recognize what Jesus did: that He loved us so much He gave His only Son to die on a cross. John 3:16: "For God so loved the world, that He gave His only begotten Son, that whosoever believes in Him should not perish, but have everlasting life."

Second, we must repent for our sins. Luke 13:3: "Unless you repent, you will perish."

It's not enough to be sorry; repentance is that turnabout from sin that is emphasized. Turn away from your old life and walk in a different direction.

Third, we must receive Jesus Christ as Savior and Lord. John 1:12: "But as many as received Him, to them He gave the right to become children of God, even to those that believe in His name."

This means that you cease trying to save yourself and accept Christ as your Lord and Savior. Trust Him completely.

Fourth, we must confess Christ publicly. Matthew 10:32: "Everyone therefore who shall confess Me before men, I will confess him before My Father who is in heaven."

It is extremely important that when you receive Christ you tell someone else about it as soon as possible. This gives you strength and courage to witness. This is what we need to know before we take our last breath.

Second Corinthians 6:2: "I tell you, now is the time of God's favor, now is the day of salvation."

As the Church, we must share this message with the world. God is knocking at your heart's door. I beg you to answer the knock. It will be the greatest decision you will ever make.

Challenge for today: Pray this prayer: "Lord, I acknowledge that I have sinned against You. I am so sorry for my sin. I am willing to turn from that old life. I openly receive and acknowledge Jesus Christ as my Savior. I confess You as Lord. From this moment on I want to live for You. Amen." Then go and tell someone. God bless you and your family today.

Isolated

We are living in some crazy times. We are living a life of isolation (pandemic), and the social butterflies of the world are having a tough time. Many of you are seeing the same family members 24 hours a day, and are not able to see your friends, and your church family. For the first time in my life, I ordered groceries to be delivered to the house. To those who are frustrated, irritated, or just ready to move past all of this, Paul has a good word for us.

Romans 12:9-13: "Love must be sincere. Hate what is evil; cling to what is good. Be devoted to one another in brotherly love. Honor one another above yourself. Never be lacking in zeal, but keep your spiritual fervor, serving the Lord. Be joyful in hope, patient in affliction, faithful in prayers. Share with God's people who are in need."

I encourage you to focus on three things today as you live this life of isolation.
1. Be joyful in hope. Be cheerfully expectant. Look for the good in each other and every situation. Learn to laugh and enjoy the simple things and odd conversations. Know that God has it all under control.
2. Be patient in affliction. This is a hard one for me. Don't be so uptight and ready to fix everything. Sit back and let God go before you. Don't quit in the hard times. Do more listening than talking. Patience is a virtue.
3. Stay faithful in prayer. Prayer needs to be a bigger part of your life. During this time of isolation reestablish your prayer life with your Heavenly Father. Carry every concern, worry, and fear to Him. Be faithful in your prayer life.

Challenge for today: Ask the Lord to fill you with joy, in Jesus' name. Take time to thank God for three things, but also think of a way you can encourage someone close to you.

Impossible/Possible

In Matthew 19:26 Jesus tells His disciples this, "With man this is impossible, but with God all things are possible."

Sometimes God shows up, and other times God just blows us away. Thirty-four miracles are recorded in the four gospels, while countless more went unrecorded. God wants to do now what He did then. Here is my question: Do you need a miracle in your life today? Do you need a special touch of faith, healing in your body, or for a family member to turn their life around? If so, don't seek a miracle, but follow hard after Jesus. If you follow Jesus long enough and far enough, you'll eventually find yourself in the middle of a mighty work of God. Keep in mind, the prerequisite for a miracle is a problem, and the bigger the problem, the greater the potential miracle. Guess what? We are all walking through the same difficulty today, and it is not easy facing hard times. In my 55 years of life, I have never seen anything like this. But in times like this, God does His best work.

No matter what you are walking through today, hold on to First Peter 5:7: "Cast all your anxiety on him because he cares for you."

This verse doesn't just tell us to cast our cares on God; it tells us why we can cast our cares on Him. He cares for you. Are you convinced that God cares for you? Until you are convinced, you will never cast your cares on Him. Trust Him. He will not turn His back on you, and He wants to do the impossible through you.

Challenge for today: I encourage you to stay strong and seek God with all your heart. Keep your spiritual eyes open for opportunities to share your faith and passion. He is the God who can make your impossible possible. He is the Way-Maker, the Miracle Worker, and the Promise Keeper. Seek His presence today.

Is It Ok to Ask God Why?

To me, one of the coolest names in the Bible is Habakkuk. Habakkuk means "to embrace or cling to". He was a minor prophet in the Old Testament, and he had a great love for his people. He had questions and doubts that came up from his jealousy for the holiness and justice of God. The prophet was perplexed over God's permission of evil in Judah, and even more so over God's use of Babylon as a rod of correction for His people.

Habakkuk 1:2-4: "How long, O Lord, must I call for help, but you do not listen? Or cry out to you, 'Violence!' but you do not save? Why do you make me look at injustice? Why do you tolerate wrong? Destruction and violence are before me; there is strife, and conflict abounds. Therefore, the law is paralyzed, and justice never prevails. The wicked hem in the righteous, so that justice is perverted."

Can you sense Habakkuk's frustration? Have you ever been as frustrated and confused by God as Habakkuk was? Here is the truth: a faith that asks God questions is a faith that is growing. God knew Habakkuk's heart, and He knew how much he loved his people. God responded back to Habakkuk with an unexpected answer in Habakkuk 1:5: "Look at the nation and watch-and be utterly amazed. For I am going to do something in your days that you would not believe, even if I told you."

We really don't understand God's ways and timing, especially when things don't go our way. It's ok to ask God questions, especially when we are struggling. We are living in tough times, and so many times we feel as though evil is winning out. I encourage you to hang in there and trust the Lord with all your heart. Don't be afraid to have real conversations with the Lord. But know this, God is at work, and He is preparing for a great harvest. I believe He is about to do something that will blow us all away. Church, keep praying, keep trusting, and keep believing. Our God is in control.

Challenge for today: Don't be afraid to ask God questions. Ask Him to give you clarity and understanding during the crazy times of life. When something doesn't make sense, go to Him and seek His guidance. Dig into God's Word and spend extra time in one-on-one conversation with God. It's ok to ask, "Why?"

Information or Transformation?

In John 14:1-4 Jesus said, "Do not let your hearts be troubled. Trust in God, trust also in me. In my Father's house are many mansions, if it were not so, I would have told you. And if I go and prepare a place for you, I will come back and take you to be with me so that you also may be where I am. You know the way to the place where I am going."

Heaven is a prepared place for a prepared person. My question is, have you given your all to Jesus Christ? Most people will miss heaven by 14 inches. The distance between your head and your heart, but it is the difference between information and transformation. It's not enough to invite Jesus into your mind. You must open the door to your heart of hearts. No door can remain locked. Even the door to your hidden room. Jesus Christ went to the cross to break the curse of sin so you can break the cycle of sin. What have you built around your heart?

Revelation 3:20: "Here I am! I stand at the door and knock. If anyone hears my voice and opens the door, I will come in and eat with him, and he with me."

Isn't it time? It's time to answer the knock at your heart's door. Time to open the door and invite Jesus in today. You will never be the same. Jesus' desire is to sit on the throne of your heart and take first place in your life.

Challenge for today: Ask yourself these questions: What is most important to me? What do I spend most of my time and energy pursuing? Who or what is sitting on the throne of your heart? Make a commitment to give Him first place and be willing to die to selfishness. He is either Lord of all or not Lord at all.

My Father Has Big Guns

My father is and always will be my hero. Growing up, he was always a constant in my life. He never missed a game and rarely ever missed a practice. Not only was he a great dad to me, but he also always took up time with my buddies who didn't have a dad. Growing up, we had a set of concrete weights with a metal bar. My brother and I would mess around with them in the yard. I remember loading up the bar with 110 lbs. and trying to dead lift it. We were getting it done. It was all I could do to pull that weight to my waist. Then my dad showed up and said, "I can pick that up with one hand over my head." There was no way. He bent over and grabbed that long bar with 110 lbs. of concrete weight. Then he let out a loud grunt and threw that weight over his head. At that point in my life, I pictured him as Superman. You see, my dad had guns (big biceps). As a child, when I was with my dad, I feared nothing. I knew he was watching over me, and I knew he would protect me no matter what. I was in the presence of a superhero.

While we are living life in a world of uncertainty, we tend to walk in fear. Businesses are closing their doors, people are losing their jobs, and you are wondering if you will get "the virus". So many negative thoughts are running through our minds. The author of Psalm 91 speaks of a place of security that I want to share with you today. Psalm 91:1-4: "He who dwells in the shelter of the Most High will rest in the shadow of the Almighty. I will say of the Lord, 'He is my refuge and my fortress, my God, in whom I trust.' Surely, he will save you from the fowler's snare and from the deadly pestilence. He will cover you with his feathers, and under his wings you will find refuge; his faithfulness will be your shield and rampart."

Challenge for today: Sit down in the presence of the Mighty God, and hand Him your worries and fears. Say this: "God you are my refuge, I trust in you, and I am safe. You rescue me from hidden traps and shield me from deadly hazards. Your huge, outstretched arms protect me. Under them I am perfectly safe." Your Heavenly Father has the "Big Guns." Fear nothing while you are walking in the presence of God. Stay positive and turn your attention to the God of the universe.

A Great White Throne

Revelation 20:11-15: "Then I saw a great white throne and him who was seated on it. Earth and sky fled from his presence, and there was no place for them. And I saw the dead, great and small, standing before the throne, and books were opened, which is the book of life. The dead were judged according to what they have done as recorded in the books. The sea gave up the dead that were in it, and each person was judged according to what he had done. Then death and Hades were thrown into the lake of fire. The lake of fire is the second death. If anyone's name was not found written in the book of life, he was thrown into the lake of fire."

I am not all about fire and brimstone, but I do want to share the truth with you. My thinking is this: It is better to hear the truth now than finding out about it too late.

In Matthew 7:21-23 Jesus says, "Not everyone who says to me, 'Lord, Lord,' will enter the kingdom of heaven, but only he who does the will of my Father who is in heaven. Many will say to me on that day, 'Lord, Lord, did we not prophesy in your name, and in your name drive out demons and perform many miracles?' Then I will tell them plainly, 'I never knew you. Away from me, you evildoers.'"

When judgment is finished, all those without Christ will be cast into hell. This is the second death. Many people reject the biblical doctrine of hell as being "unchristian," and yet Jesus clearly taught its reality. (Matthew 18:8; 23:15; 33; 25:46; Mark 9:46) A sentimental kind of humanistic religion will not face the reality of judgment but teaches about a God who loves everyone into heaven and sends no one to hell. Hell is a witness to the righteous character of God. He must judge sin. Hell is also a witness of man's responsibility. The fact is man is not a robot or a helpless victim, but a creature able to make choices. Hell is also a witness to the awfulness of sin. If we see sin as God sees it, we will understand why a place like hell exists. In the light of Calvary, no lost person can condemn God for casting them into hell. God has provided a way of escape in a relationship with Jesus Christ. God will not lower His standards or alter His requirements. He has ordained that faith in His Son is the only way of salvation.

The White Throne Judgment will be nothing like our modern-day court cases. At the White Throne, there will be a Judge but no jury, a prosecutor but no defense, and a sentence, but no appeal.

Challenge for today: Think about these three questions and answer them. Have you ever given your heart to Jesus Christ? What evidence can be found that you made that decision? Are you prepared to stand before a Holy God? You may not believe any of this, but it doesn't stop it from being true.

The Unexpected

There are things in life that come unexpected. Things happen that you cannot understand, explain, or prepare for. Hitting a deer with your car is one of those things. No matter how cautious you are or how carefully you look, that deer will pop out from nowhere. Then it's too late to react. How about when you come home for lunch, like you do every day, to find your home has been burglarized. All your valuables and things you really appreciate are gone. How do you prepare for that? Why my house? How about when a virus comes, and people are dying around you? Businesses are closing, family and friends are losing their jobs, and fear enters your life. I remember calling the Covid Virus a hoax. Boy was I wrong. When the unexpected happens, be prepared.

I don't share this to scare you or frighten you into a relationship with Jesus. But I want to share the truth with you. Second Peter 3:10-14: "But the day of the Lord will come like a thief. The heavens will disappear with a roar; the elements will be destroyed by fire, and the earth and everything in it will be laid bare. Since everything will be destroyed in this way, what kind of people ought you to be? You ought to live holy, and godly lives as you look forward to the day of the Lord and expect His coming. That day will be the destruction of heaven by fire, and the elements will melt in the heat. But in keeping with his promise, we are looking forward to a new heaven and a new earth, the home of righteousness. So then, dear friend, since you are looking at this, make every effort to be found spotless, blameless, and at peace with him."

Talk about the unexpected. Like a thief in the night, or a deer hitting your car, or a pandemic happening all over the world, Jesus will come again. Can you explain it, understand it, or even comprehend it? No. But it's going to happen. Are you prepared?

Jesus said in John 14:1-4, "Do not let your hearts be troubled. Trust in God, trust also in me. In my Father's house are many mansions; if it were not so, I would have told you. I am going there to prepare a place for you. And if I go and prepare a place for you, I will come back and take you to be with me so that you also may be where I am. You know the way to the place where I am going."

Some people may call it a hoax, but that doesn't stop it from being true. Heaven is a prepared place for a prepared person. The unexpected is going to happen. Will you be ready? Jesus said in John 14:6: "I am the way and the truth and the life. No one comes to the Father except through me." Accepting Jesus as your Lord and Savior is the only way to be prepared for the unexpected. God bless you and your family.

Challenge for today: Stop and ask yourself these questions: Are you fully confident about your eternal destination? Can you explain why you feel the way you do about that destination? When you think about family, is there someone you love that needs to hear this message of love and forgiveness? You and the ones you love must be prepared for the unexpected.

God's Warning to Us

Moses received a powerful word from the Lord that I need today. Deuteronomy 8:1-2: "Be careful to follow every command I am giving you today, so that you may live and increase and may enter and possess the land that the Lord promised an oath to your forefathers. Remember how the Lord your God led you all the way in the desert for forty years, to humble you and test you to know what was in your heart."

God called Israel to complete obedience. This obedience was based on remembering what God had done for them in the wilderness. God brought Israel to a place where they had to be totally dependent on the Lord. Moses needed to look back with gratefulness and remember how faithful God was to him and Israel. How has God shown you faithfulness over the years?

Deuteronomy 8:6-7: "Observe the commands of the Lord your God, walking in his ways and revering him. For the Lord your God is bringing you into a good land."

Not only did Moses look back with gratefulness, but he also moved forward in obedience. He focused on every word that came from the mouth of the Lord. God blesses obedience. God is calling the United States of America back to a place of obedience. We need to look back to the faithfulness of the Lord and remember how this country began. We need to fall on our face before a Holy God and repent of our wicked ways. Then begin to walk in obedience pushing aside selfish pride and wayward hearts.

I want to leave you with this final thought. Deuteronomy 8:19-20: "If you ever forget the Lord your God and follow other gods and worship and bow down to them, I testify against you today that you will surely be destroyed. Like the nations that the Lord destroyed before you, so you will be destroyed for not obeying the Lord your God."

Who will you serve? Will you repent and fall on our knees before the Lord? Or will you turn your backs to Him and follow your own wicked ways? For me and my house, we will serve the Lord. God is calling us to look back and see His faithfulness over the years. Move forward in obedience and follow hard after Him. Wake up Church.

Challenge for today: Pray daily for this nation. Pray over our national, state, and local leaders. Pray that there will be a spirit of repentance that falls over our country. As a nation, pray that we will go back to the faith that built this country and that we will return to God. Pray and believe.

No Turning Back

I wanted to share scripture from the Old Testament. Before I do, you need to know for sure that God is in control, and He loves you very much. Let the world see the love of God in your heart. First Kings 19:19-21: "So Elijah went from there and found Elisha son of Shaphat. He was plowing with twelve yokes of oxen, and he himself was driving the twelfth pair. Elijah went up to him and threw his cloak around him. Elisha then left his oxen and ran after Elijah. 'Let me kiss my father and my mother good-bye,' he said, 'and then I will come with you.' 'Go back,' Elijah replied. 'What have I done to you?' So, Elisha left him and went back. He took his yoke of oxen and slaughtered them. He burned the plowing equipment to cook the meat and gave it to the people, and they ate. Then he set out to follow Elijah and became his attendant."

To say the least, Elisha was all in. How easy would it have been for Elisha to come up with a list of excuses because he couldn't follow Elijah.

There is an old hymn that I love to sing, and it has so much personal meaning to me. It goes something like this: "I have decided to follow Jesus, I have decided to follow Jesus, I have decided to follow Jesus, no turning back, no turning back." It's time to go all in with Jesus Christ.

Challenge for today: Answer the Father's call and be obedient to what God is calling you to do. Keep your spiritual eyes and ears open, and don't make any excuses. Watch for opportunities that God may put in front of you. It may overwhelm you, but learn how to trust Him. He loves to take you out of your comfort zone. Go all in. No turning back.

What Matters

Psalm 90:12: "So teach us to number our days so that we may gain a heart of wisdom."

I grew up loving to play sports. But to me, the best part about playing sports was getting a trophy. It was all about the hardware. I wanted trophies to cover the walls of my room. Every time I would fill up a shelf with trophies, my dad would make another shelf to display them all. Those trophies meant the world to me. A trophy meant success to me. Life happens and other things will become much more important than some old trophies. All my trophies ended up in a box and eventually got thrown in a dumpster. So, what really matters?

Who you love and who loves you? That is what really matters, the love between you, God, and those He places close in your life. It's also about time. What are you doing with it? James 4:14: "Why, you don't even know what will happen tomorrow. What is your life? You are a mist that appears for a little while and then vanishes away."

Our life is like a vanishing vapor. Here one moment, then gone the next. God does have a purpose for each one of us in our short stay here. Here is the question of the day: What have you been giving your heart to lately? Our time here with family and friends is fleeting. Ephesians 5:15-17: "Be very careful, then, how you live-not as unwise but as wise, make the most of every opportunity, because the days are evil. Therefore, do not be foolish, but understand what the Lord's will is."

Challenge for today: Make the most of every opportunity the Lord brings before you. Make it count. What are you investing in? Who are you investing in? Block out time each week to spend with people who mean the world to you. What can you do today that will put a smile on someone's face?

Keep Fighting

Second Corinthians 4:8-9: "We are hard pressed on every side, but not crushed; perplexed, but not in despair; persecuted, but not abandoned, struck down, but not destroyed."

We who are in Christ will face hardships, trials, and suffering in our lives. God will take you through tough times of training and use them to bring about His character. How we respond to them reflects our trust in Him to produce character and perseverance.

David was a man who knew how to take a punch. He wrote Psalm 25:16-21 and said, "Turn to me and be gracious to me, for I am lonely and afflicted. The troubles of my heart have multiplied; free me from my anguish. Look upon my affliction and my distress and take away my sins. See how my enemies have increased and how fiercely they hate me! Guard my life and rescue me; let me not be put to shame, for I take refuge in you. May integrity and uprightness protect me, because my hope is in you."

During David's pain and suffering, he always knew he belonged to God. What got him through all these difficult situations? His strength was not found in himself, his money, or his possessions, and it certainly was not in the people around him. His strength was found in the Lord. His hope was found in his relationship with the Lord.

We are all going to get knocked down sooner or later. We will all face frustrations and let downs in this life. Our biggest battle is to believe God is with us when trials show up at our doorstep. During these times, we tend to get down, get overwhelmed, be bitter, and ask why. During these times, we must keep fighting. We must set our feet, take courage, and choose to believe God is real and alive and working out His purpose in us.

Challenge for today: Define your struggle. What is it that is beating you up and leaving you overwhelmed? Embrace your struggles, and then give them all to the Lord. Let Him go before you and fight for you. Trust Him with it all. When you get knocked down, get up, and keep fighting.

The Secret Place

I want to share a short word with you, and I pray you will receive this message. Jesus said in Matthew 6:6: "But when you pray, go into your room, close the door and pray to your Father, who is unseen. Then your Father, who sees what is done in secret, will reward you."

You can tell those people who pray in secret. They shine with the very glory of God. They seem to have a humble boldness about them, a gentle strength, and a quiet confidence. But for most of us, the pace of this life kills our prayer life. Finding time to pray, much less a "secret place" is hard to do with all that we have going on. Jesus understood this, Luke 5:15-16: "Yet the news about him spread all the more, so the crowd of people came near to him and to be healed of their sickness. But Jesus often withdrew to lonely places and prayed."

The secret place is where it is just you and God. It's a place away from every distraction. A place where there is no show and tell. No fancy words used to impress others. It's just you and the Creator of the world where all pretense is gone. If Jesus needed this secret place, how much more do we need to get away and pray? Make room for God in your life. "Lord, help us to find that secret place where we can push aside the business of life. I worship and praise your holy name."

Challenge for today: Where can you go to get away from everything? What time of day do you seem to be your sharpest? Set that time and place to meet along with the King. Then make a commitment to God and tell Him your intentions. One more thing, leave your phone behind. Just you and God. You will find out that you can survive without that cell phone.

Why Am I Here?

Colossians 1:16: "For by him all things were created: things in heaven and on earth, visible and invisible, whether thrones or powers or rulers or authorities; all things were created by him and for him. Have you ever asked yourself, 'Why am I Here?' You were created by Jesus Christ and for Jesus Christ. You will have a hole in your heart until you belong to Jesus Christ. The one relationship you cannot do without is a personal relationship with the God who created you. Just know, God loves you very much, and He wants to be in a close love relationship with you. We were created to live 'for Him.'"

But Isaiah 53:6 tells us this, "We all, like sheep, have gone astray, each of us has turned to his own way."

To be straight forward, we are running a life that God is supposed to run, and God calls this sin. Sin is the root of selfishness, loneliness, and guilt in our lives. We are trying to live without the love and the life that we were created for; a life only God can give. Most of us know there's something between us and God. That's why we try to do good things to get to Him. But doing good can never satisfy the penalty of sin. Ephesians 2:8-9: "For it is by grace you have been saved, through faith-and this not from yourself, it is a gift of God-not by works, so that no one can boast."

The Good News is that even though we did the sinning, Jesus did the dying to pay our death penalty for our sins when He died on the cross. He was buried in a borrowed tomb, but three days later Jesus arose from the grave. Jesus is alive and well, and He lives in my heart. Praise God. John 3:16: "For God so loved the world that he gave his one and only Son, that whoever believes in him shall not perish but have eternal life."

The most important decision you will ever make is what to do with Jesus. It's a relationship you must choose.

Challenge for today: Will you choose Him today? Take time to thank God for His grace and mercy. We can never thank Him enough. Stop long enough to reflect on the pain that Jesus suffered for us when He was beaten half to death. See His face when He took those nails to the wrist and feet on that rugged cross. Celebrate Jesus today.

You Have a Choice/Choose Well

Joshua wrote Joshua 24:14–15: "Now fear the Lord and serve him with faithfulness. Throw away the gods your forefathers worship beyond the River and in Egypt, and serve the Lord. But if serving the Lord seems undesirable to you, then choose for yourselves this day whom you will serve, whether the gods your forefathers served beyond the River, or the god of the Amorites, in whose land you are living. But as for me and my house, we will serve the Lord."

He wasn't done yet, Joshua 24:19-20: "Joshua said to the people, 'You are not able to serve the Lord. He is a Holy God; he is a jealous God. He will not forgive your rebellion and sin. If you forsake the Lord and serve foreign gods, he will turn and bring disaster on you and make an end to you, after he has been good to you.'"

But in verse 31 the people said to Joshua, "No! We will serve the Lord."

They made their choice. Joshua closes out and writes Joshua 24:23-24: "Throw away the foreign gods that are among you and yield your hearts to the Lord, the God of Israel." And the people said to Joshua, "We will serve the Lord our God and obey him."

Jesus speaks in Revelation 22:12-13: "Behold, I am coming soon. My reward is with me, and I will give to everyone according to what he has done. I am the Alpha and the Omega, the First and the Last, the Beginning and the End."

You have a choice how you live your life, choose well. So many times, in life we get our priorities out of whack. It is so easy to worship the created and not the Creator. Return to your first love. Run to the Savior and fall at His feet. Get your heart right and confess your sins to Him. Throw away the foreign gods and yield your heart to the Lord. Stop long enough to listen to what God is trying to tell you. God bless and choose well because we all are going to be accountable for how we live.

Challenge for today: When you make any decisions, don't make them in haste. Take time to think things through and take time to pray about them. Run them past your Heavenly Father and see what He has to say about it all. Even take time to run it all by a trusted friend.

Tear Down/Build Up/Be Obedient

In Judges 6:24, Gideon built an altar to the Lord and called it "The Lord is Peace". Many people around the world need this very thing in their lives. They are looking for peace in the middle of a crazy storm. Let's take a quick look at what Gideon did to reclaim peace in his life. Peace is not having a lot of money, a great job, or having a huge house, and a fancy car. All that stuff will not give you true happiness. All that can be destroyed or lost in a blink of an eye.

Judges 6:25-27: "That same night the Lord said to him, 'Take the second bull from your father's herd, the one seven-year-old. Tear down your father's altar to Baal and cut down the Asherah pole beside it. Then build a proper kind of altar to the Lord your God on the top of this height. Using the wood of the Asherah pole that you cut down, offer the second bull as a burnt offering.' So Gideon took ten of his servants and did as the Lord told him."

I want to put this in the simplest form. If you are looking for true peace in your life, there are three things you will have to do.

First, tear down the idols that you have built up over the years. Idols are anything you love more than God. What is that in your life? It may be an object like a house, boat, or a truck. It may be a passion or hobby like fishing, sports, or even shopping. Tear it down.

Second, rebuild your altar of God. Renew your love relationship with the Father. Confess your sins to Him, ask for forgiveness, and pursue His presence. Take time to enjoy your fellowship with God.

Third, be obedient to what He places in front of you. When we begin to walk in fellowship with God, He will start showing you incredible things He wants you to do. He knows your talents because He is the One who gave them to you. God blesses obedience. Be willing to say yes. The Lord gives peace that only He can give. Burn up the idols of your heart, rebuild the altar of God, and be obedient to what He calls you to do.

Challenge for today: Set aside extra time to get real with God. Identify those things in your life that are more important than your relationship with Him. Take time to confess those sins and tell God you are sorry. After a time of confession, identify your talents and passions. Are you using your talents to glorify your Heavenly Father? What is He calling you to do? When He shows you what it is, be obedient.

Waiting In the Right Place

Acts 1:4-5: "On one occasion, while he was eating with them, he gave them a command: 'Do not leave Jerusalem but wait for the gift my Father promised, which you have heard me speak about. For John baptized with water, but in a few days, you will be baptized with the Holy Spirit.'"

After Jesus' resurrection, He spent 40 days with His disciples, teaching them, encouraging them, and equipping them. At one of their gatherings, He told them to wait in Jerusalem, and they would receive the power of the Holy Spirit. In Acts 1:13-14, we see that the disciples were obedient to what Jesus told them to do. They gathered in one place, and they prayed constantly. For ten days the disciples prayed together. They were waiting in a place of obedience.

In Acts 2:1-4, because of their obedience, they received the gift of the Holy Spirit. Doubters became prophets, and frightened men and women became bold. Peter preached like never before. People came, and God opened the floodgate on the greatest movement in history. It all began because the followers of Jesus were willing to wait in the right place. The place of obedience. They waited in the right place for power. Waiting means watching for Him. If you are waiting on God, you are watching for God. If you're waiting on God, you are searching for God. If you are waiting on God, you are hoping in God. Waiting also means working through conflict, forgiving others, and resolving disputes. Ten days of praying and a few moments of preaching led to 3,000 people coming to Christ. Are we guilty of preaching for ten days and praying for a few minutes?

Challenge for today: Wait on Him, but make sure you wait in the right place, the place of obedience. During this crazy time, God has taken away so many distractions and idols in our lives. Now we have time to get our lives back in tune with Him. Get real and honest with God today. Take time to share your heart with the One who loves you the most. But also get things right in your relationships around you. Wait in the place of obedience because God is about to swing open the doors of ministry. There is a reason for all this waiting.

I Will Not Be Afraid

Psalm 118:1-6: "Give thanks to the Lord, for he is good; his love endures forever. Let Israel say: 'His love endures forever.' Let the house of Aaron say: 'His love endures forever.' Let those who fear the Lord say: 'His love endures forever.' In my anguish I cry to the Lord, and he answers by setting me free. The Lord is with me; I will not be afraid." Rise-up Church. Do not be afraid, the Lord is with us.

When the things of this world overcome us, we can become overwhelmed, frustrated, and full of anxiety. There will be times in this life when we will feel all alone, and we feel like the weight of the world rests on our shoulders. If you are anything like me, you try to be strong and tough, and you do your very best to keep marching forward. Sickness and death may stare you in the face. Death and sadness will rise on every side. Depression will fall over you when you least expect it. Satan will throw every temptation at you including the kitchen sink. Enemies will rise-up and try their best to destroy you. Shame and regret will fill your mind with lies and deceit. We are right in a spiritual war zone with bombs going off all around us. Does that sound anything like your life?

When things seem to be falling apart all around you, don't be afraid. We have a God who loves us and has given everything we need to overcome. Paul tells us this in Second Timothy 1:7: "For God hasn't given us a spirit of fear, but a spirit of power, of love and self-discipline."

That is a promise of God Himself, and we need to stand on that truth. In these difficult times, stop and give thanks to your Heavenly Father. Take your eyes off the negative and turn your focus to an all-powerful and loving God. Know this, He is still in control, and He has your best interest in mind. Fear the Lord, not the distraction around you, and He will give you peace.

Challenge for today: Overcome those fears that have been haunting you for years. Face them head on and don't run from them. Know that our God is for you, not against you. No matter what trouble, situation, or sickness you face, know that He is greater. When things begin to overwhelm you, stop and say, "The Lord is with me: I will not be afraid." There is victory in Jesus.

The Rescue

It is my heart and my passion to share with you the encouragement that the Lord gives me every day. During these times of uncertainties, I encourage you to dive deep with the Lord. Don't sit in fear and worry but open the Word and worship. Put your hope and trust in the One who is in control. His name is Jesus.

Let's look at the nugget of truth that God gives us in Second Corinthians 1:3-6. Paul writes, "Praise be to the God and Father of our Lord Jesus Christ, the Father of compassion and the God of all comfort, who comforts in all our troubles, so that we can comfort those in any trouble with the comfort we ourselves have received from God. For just as the sufferings of Christ flows over into our lives, so also through Christ our comfort overflows. If we are distressed, it is for your comfort and salvation; if we are comforted, it is for your comfort, which produces in you patient endurance of the same suffering we suffer. And our hope for you is firm, because we know that just as you share in our sufferings; so also you share in our comfort."

All praise to the God of heaven and earth. He is the Father of all mercy. He comes alongside us when we go through hard times, and before you know it, He brings us alongside someone else who needs that same encouragement that we just received from the Father. We are all out of our comfort zones and our world is in a frenzy, but God is opening the doors of ministry all over the world. Let the world see the overflow of our hearts of comfort, peace, and love. Just as Christ has come alongside you, pull up beside someone who needs comforting or encouraging. It's time for the Church to be what God designed us to be. God is calling us to be hope dealers and to share His message of Jesus Christ with those around us. "Lord, open our eyes to see what You see and let us be willing to do something about it."

Challenge for today: First, thank God for His faithfulness and His comforting love He has shown us over and over again. Thank Him for those times He showed you grace, and He stepped into a difficult situation and held your hand. Second, take time to look around and notice other people who are hurting or struggling in life. Be that voice of encouragement and be willing to share what God has freely shared with you.

Do We Want Healing?

This world is a crazy place. It is full of deceit, brokenness, and pain. Things are happening that I have never seen before. But when things get crazy in this world, God seems to do His greatest work. But through it all, God is in control. "Lord, help me not to complain and grumble, but show me how we can encourage others, and be a part of what you are doing."

There are four things God calls His Church to do today. Be humble and kick selfish pride to the curb. We need to take "self" off the throne of our hearts.

1. We need to pray like we have never prayed before. There is a spiritual war going on, and we need to unite and pray for healing and revival.
2. We need to seek His face and not His hands.
3. We need to run to God and desire His presence more than anything.
4. We need to repent. We need to fall on our faces before God and confess our sins. It is time that we get real with Him and take care of our filthy hearts.

Second Chronicles 7:14: "If my people, who are called by my name, will humble themselves and pray and seek my face and turn from their wicked ways, then will I hear from heaven and will forgive their sins and will heal their land."

We have a choice; to be obedient or do our own thing. We need healing. Our nation needs healing. Our world needs healing - not from the Coronavirus but from sin. This scripture ends with a promise. If the Church does their part, then God will do a glorious work. He will forgive our sins and heal our land. God always backs up His promises. We must do our part.

Challenge for today: Ask God to reveal your true heart. Then wait and see what He shows you. Whatever it is, deal with it right here and now. Don't put it off. Spend time talking it out with the Lord. Get to the root of that sin and give it to Jesus. Then pray for this country and pray that the heart of the people would turn back to the one true God.

Good News

Do you need to hear something that is positive and encouraging? Are you tired of hearing negative, destructive, and depressing words? I don't know about you, but I need some good news. If you have a second, let's dive into God's Word. I hope you can receive this and soak in it all day.

Romans 8:35-39: "Who shall separate us from the love of Christ? Shall trouble or hardship or persecution or famine or nakedness or danger or sword? As it is written: 'For your sake we face death all day long; we are considered as sheep to be slaughtered.' No, in all these things we are more than conquerors through him who loved us. For I am convinced that neither death nor life, neither angels nor demons, neither the present nor the future, nor any powers, neither height nor depth, nor anything else in all creation, will be able to separate us from the love of God that is in Christ Jesus our Lord."

That's the good news we need to spread today. We are loved by the King of kings, and no matter what we come against, His love for us never changes and His love never runs out. Are you convinced that God cares for you? Until you are convinced, you will never cast your cares on Him. You are a conqueror, a mighty warrior, and a child of the living God. Heads up Church. It's time to move forward, stay positive, and share His good news with the world.

Challenge for today: Memorize Romans 8:35-39. When this world tries to beat you down, and when negativity surrounds you, quote this verse out loud. Say it over and over again. Reassure yourself that you are a conqueror in Christ, and nothing will separate you from Him.

Reassuring Hope

We live in a world of uncertainty. Stocks can be soaring one day and drop 2000 points the next day. Retirement was just around the corner, but now it might be pushed out a couple of years. You can be completely healthy today and fight for your life next year. That job you had for over 20 years just gave you the pink slip. How in the world will you put food on your table and pay your bills? That person you leaned on for so many years just passed away. In this world of uncertainty, there is something that never changes. God's love for us and His Word will never fade, never fail us, and never change. In hard times, and in times of uncertainty turn to the Rock of your salvation.

I want to give you some reassuring hope found in God's love letter to us. Psalm 27:1-3: "The Lord is my light and my salvation-whom shall I fear? The Lord is my stronghold of my life, of whom shall I be afraid. When evil men advance me to devour my flesh, when my enemies and my foes attack me, they will stumble and fall. Though an army besiege me, my heart will not fear; though war breaks out against me, even then I will be confident."

When fear overcomes you, hold on to Isaiah 43:1-3: "Fear not, for I have redeemed you; I have summoned you by name; you are mine. When you pass through the waters, I will be with you; and when you pass through the rivers, they will not sweep over you. When you walk through the fire, you will not be burned; the flames will not set you ablaze. For I am the Lord, your God, the Holy One of Israel, your Savior."

Hold on to Psalm 121:1-8: "I lift up my eyes to the hills-where does my help come from? My help comes from the Lord, the Maker of heaven and earth. He will not let your foot slip-he who watches over you will never slumber; indeed, he who watches over Israel will never slumber or sleep. The Lord watches over you-he the Lord is your shade at your right hand; the sun will not harm you by day, nor the moon by night. The Lord will keep you from harm-he will watch over your life; the Lord will watch over your coming and going both now and forevermore."

Challenge for today: God has a plan. He is never surprised. God didn't save Daniel from the lion's den, but He saved him in the lion's den. He doesn't get us out, he gets us through. Sometimes we just need to turn off the TV and open God's Word. He cares about you, and He loves you. Put your trust in the hands of the loving Father. Choose hope and not fear today.

Do Not Fear

As you read these scriptures, please ask the Lord to give you understanding and discernment. Let God's Word go deep, and let it take root in your life. Moses told the people to strap the scriptures on their heads. Do this with today's word. God has a robe of peace that He wants to put around you today.

Lamentations 3:55-57: "I call on your name, O Lord, from the depths of the pit. You heard my plea: 'Do not close your ears to my cry for relief.' You came near when I called you, and you said, 'Do not fear.'"

Psalm 42:11: "Why are you downcast, O my soul? Why so disturbed within me? Put your Hope in God, for I will yet praise him, my Savior and my God."

Psalm 91:2: "I will say of the Lord, 'He is my refuge and my fortress, my God, in whom I trust.'"

There is so much going on in our world today. So many are turning their ears to the news, and all the ruckus that is going on around us, when we should be turning our attention to the Lord. I want to put this in the most simplistic words. Do not fear. Place your trust in the One who owns it all. He is my refuge, my high tower, and my fortress. When I was a child, I used to jump to my dad from the top step when he got home from work. I was not afraid because I knew he would catch me every time. Take your eyes off fear and uncertainty placing them on the Savior of the world. He is there to catch you. Giving in to fear will leave you empty and without hope. "Lord, cover me and your Church with your robe of peace and hope today. I pray that fear will not overcome us. My trust is in you Lord. Amen."

Challenge for today: Read and memorize 1 Peter 5:7: "Cast all your anxiety on him because he cares for you."

Are you convinced that God cares for you? Until you are convinced, you will never cast your cares on Him. Know this, He is bigger than all your fears. Trust Him and let Him carry that heavy load. He will catch you from the top step.

God's There

Another day to serve the Holy God of heaven. Make every day count. Psalm 145:17-21: "The Lord is righteous in all his ways and loving towards all he has made. The Lord is near to all who call on him, to all who call on him in truth. He fulfills the desires of those who fear him; he hears their cry and saves them. The Lord watches over all who love him, but all the wicked he will destroy. My mouth will speak in praise of the Lord. Let every creature praise his holy name forever and ever."

Do you remember when you were in school, and you were handed a test back with lots of red ink? Oh, the mistakes we have made. Think about it, everything God does is right and perfect. The trademark on all his work is love. He is there, listening to all who pray and call out to Him. He hears our cries. He feels our hurts, and He understands what we go through every day. He always does what is best for those who fear Him. God sticks by all who love Him. Let our mouth be full of God's praise today. Let everything that is living bless Him forever and ever. We all know that life isn't always peaches and cream; there will be times of frustration, disappointment, and hurt. Through it all, whether it is good or bad, God is there, standing by our side and loving us all the way through this life. He is there when we must make those hard decisions, and He stands by us when we feel all alone. He is there to forgive when we make mistakes. He never waivers or fails to show up when we need Him most. He is never late. Jesus experienced what it is like to live here on planet earth, and he knows that we will need all the help we can get. Know this He loves us, and He will never leave us or forsake us. His love is constant, and it will never run out.

Challenge for today: Take time throughout your day and say, "I am loved by the very Creator of heaven and earth." Keep that simple message before you and remind yourself that no matter what you face, that you are loved, and you are not alone. Look for opportunities to share His amazing love.

My Hope Is in You

It's time to worship. Jeremiah writes in Lamentations 3:22-26, "Because of the Lord's great love we are not consumed, for his compassion never fails. They are new every morning; great is your faithfulness. I say to myself, 'The Lord is my portion; therefore, I will wait for him.' The Lord is good to those whose hope is in him, to the one who seeks him. It is good to wait quietly for the salvation of the Lord."

We live in a world today where waiting is a crime. I will be the first one to admit, I hate to wait on anything. If we go out to eat on Friday night, I want to be there as close to 5:00 pm as possible. It drives my wife crazy, but we are not waiting in line for our food. We live in the world of fast food, drive throughs, and the internet is never fast enough to please us. There is nothing in life that frustrates me more than five lanes of traffic that comes to a complete stop and all you see for a mile ahead of you is brake lights. Have you ever waited for two hours to ride a roller coaster, and the ride only took five minutes? Some couples wait for years to have children. Waiting is hard, and it is frustrating. One of the toughest things to do in this life is to wait on God. I have always heard that God is never late because He is always right on time, but it does not change the fact that waiting is never fun or easy.

Jeremiah knew of God's great love, and he had experienced His faithfulness over the years. We will all have hard times and will face difficult situations. But I encourage you to rest in the Lord and trust in Him. Let Him carry your heavy load. He will never let you down. Be confident that there is a reason and purpose for your waiting. "Lord, my hope is in You."

Challenge for today: When faced with the frustration of waiting, simply tell the Lord out loud, "My hope is in You." Say it over and over all day long until you begin to believe it. We all will have to wait when it comes to living life. My question is this: how are you waiting? In that time of waiting, learn to rest in God, soaking in the love of your Heavenly Father. Dine on His truths in Scripture. Say it again, "My hope is in You."

Sifting

Luke 22:31-32: "Simon, Simon! Indeed, Satan has asked for you, that he may sift you as wheat. But I have prayed for you, that your faith should not fail."

When Satan asked to sift Peter, his purpose was not to get rid of what was undesired in order to keep the best. His purpose was to shake Peter's faith so that nothing was left. God allowed the sifting, but He had a different purpose in mind, and it made all the difference between defeat and victory. The only way we can successfully struggle through these times is to focus on the Author of Truth and not on our circumstances. While He may allow us to be tested, God has faithfully promised to never leave us or forsake us.

When one sifts flour, it is an examination of all the parts. The lumps are left in the sieve, so the product is better to eat. God has a purpose in sifting us. What is most obvious is this: God uses sifted people. God always has a plan and a purpose for what goes on in our lives. Ephesians 2:10: "For we are God's workmanship, created in Christ Jesus to do good works which God prepares for us to do."

He allows us to be sifted to bring honor and glory to Himself. God also allows us to be sifted to grow us up to be a better product. In the process of sifting us, God pushes us beyond our capabilities so that we must trust Him. You may be in the process of being sifted, and you may be in that very difficult season of life. Know this, you are not alone, God is doing a work in you. Hang on and trust Him. What is your response to His sifting? You can rebel. You can blame God. You can run, you can try your best to jump out of the sifter, OR you can let God have His way with you and surrender fully to His will.

Challenge for today: Turn to the Lord and ask for strength and wisdom. Lean on Him and receive godly counsel. Don't be afraid to ask your friends to pray for you. Sifting happens for a reason, and God has a plan for it. Trust Him; He has your best interest at heart.

Overcoming Discontentment

Sooner or later, we all struggle with discontentment. Are you bored with your job? Have the kids moved out of the house? Do you need a change in some area of your life? The apostle Paul knew something that most of us have missed. He knew how to be content in any circumstance. Paul wrote in Philippians 4:10-13: "But I rejoice in the Lord greatly, that now at last you have revived your concern for me; indeed, you were concerned before, but you lacked opportunity. Not that I speak from want; for I have learned to be content in whatever circumstances I am. I know how to get along with humble means, and I also know how to live in prosperity; in any circumstance I have learned the secret of being filled and going hungry, both of having abundance and suffering. I can do all things through Christ who strengthens me."

What is the secret to contentment? I believe it has to do with our willingness to accept three powerful truths.
1. Real contentment hinges on what's happening inside of us, not around us.
2. Know that contentment is need-oriented not want-oriented. God will meet our needs; He is going to take care of us. Much of our discontentment comes from not getting what we want.
3. Contentment is a matter of trust. Contentment is trusting God even when things seem out of control.

Challenge for today: Seek His direction in whatever season you are in. Here are five things to try when hit with discontentment.
1. Refuse to blame your circumstances.
2. Take responsibility for your feelings.
3. Admit to the Lord that you have allowed your contentment to become too attached to your circumstances.
4. Distinguish between what you need and what you want.
5. Take time to thank Him for meeting your needs. Then memorize and meditate on Philippians 4:10-13.

Guard Your Mind

Your mind is a battlefield, and Satan is on the prowl to figure out a way to bring you down. He loves to attack you with worry, negativity, and a worldly mindset. That is why Paul wrote Second Corinthians 10:3-4: "For though we live in the world, we do not wage war as the world does. The weapons we fight with are not weapons of the world. On the contrary, they have divine power to demolish strongholds."

God has given us everything we need to overcome the lies of Satan and to be victorious. Second Corinthians 10:5: "We demolish arguments and every pretension that sets itself up against the knowledge of God, and we take captive every thought to make it obedient to Christ."

You may be locked in a prison, and the only lock on the door is a lie. Capture the lies and replace them with God's truth. Truth will set you free; truth will always win. Your life is always moving in the same direction as your strongest thoughts. Think about that. In other words, you can't have a positive life with a negative mind set. I encourage you to identify the number one stronghold that is holding you back. You cannot defeat what you cannot define. Romans 12:2: "Do not conform any longer to the patterns of this world, but be transformed by the renewing of your mind. Then you will be able to test and approve what God's will is-his good, pleasing and perfect will."

I want you to name the truth that demolishes that stronghold. You are not who the enemy claims you are. You are a child of the King. You are a warrior of the Most High God. You are victorious and an overcomer through Jesus Christ our Lord. Renew your mind in Christ and stand strong.

Challenge for today: Identify the lies that are holding you captive. Write them down and look at them one by one. Now, find the truth in God's Word that exposes those lies. Ask God to make you more aware of the schemes that Satan uses to trip you up. We guard what we consider to be valuable like our home, cars, and our money. I have an alarm system in my home, and it guards my home while I am away and even when I am asleep. God's Word will guard your mind in the same way. It will send out alerts and let you know when lies pop up and when there is danger all around you that you may not even be aware of. Trust His truth and guard your mind.

Seven Things About Grace

Ephesians 1:3-8: "Praise be to the God and Father of our Lord Jesus Christ, who has blessed us in the heavenly realms with every spiritual blessing in Christ. For he chose us in him before the creation of the world to be holy and blameless in his sight. In love He predestined us to be adopted as his sons through Jesus Christ, in accordance with his pleasure and will-to the praise of his glorious grace, which he has freely given us in the One he loves. In him we have redemption through his blood, the forgiveness of sins, in accordance with the riches of God's grace that he lavished on us with all wisdom and understanding."

"Thank you, Lord."

Grace comes into our lives when we receive Jesus as our personal Savior. He frees us from the penalty of sin and the power of sin in our lives. There are seven truths found here in Ephesians 1 about the riches of God's grace:

1. The riches of the grace of God are given by God the Father.
2. These riches are freely given. That means we don't earn these riches.
3. This grace is given to us in abundance. His grace is immeasurable.
4. His grace is given instantly. He gave us grace the moment we were saved.
5. The riches of grace come simultaneously. He doesn't hold anything back to save for later.
6. The riches of grace are totally on the merit of what Jesus did, not on any of our merits.
7. His death brought the riches of grace for us. He paid the debt in full that we could not pay.

Challenge of today: The riches of grace are eternal. Money can't buy it, and death can't take it away. Shout out with joy because we have been redeemed, set free, and brought into the family of God. Wow, what a Savior!

The God of Second Chances

Ephesians 2:8-9: "For by grace you have been saved through faith, and that not of yourselves; it is the gift of God, not of works, lest anyone should boast."

Romans 3:23 tells us that all of us have messed up and fallen short. Thank goodness grace greater than our sin was offered. Think about it, most people hear the gospel many times before they receive the Lord. That is grace. He does not give up on calling us to Himself. He is persistent because He loves us so much. You see, He is the God of second chances, and oftentimes a hundred chances. He will often send someone our way to tell us about a Savior. We often reject the truth. Because He is the God of grace, He will send another to share with us again. This process could take years because we are so stubborn.

This should encourage us as believers to pray for those who do not know Christ. To that wife who has been praying for her husband to believe the Truth - don't give up. Keep praying and believing. To the parent of a wayward child, keep loving them through it all, even when you want to throw your hands up. God's grace is pursuing that son or daughter. We may give up, but God doesn't. His grace is abundant. Thank God He doesn't measure grace out in teaspoons. "Thank you, Lord, for never giving up on me. Thank you for your grace. Help me to show grace to others."

Challenge of today:
1. Take time to reflect on the grace that God has shown you over the years.
2. Say thank you and give Him the praise He is due. Yes, worship Him today.
3. Who do you need to show grace toward today? What we have received, we need to give away. Who has God put on your heart to show grace to today?

God's Plan

What is God's plan? To reach this lost and dying world? His master plan is to use the Church. In other words, He wants to use you, and there is no backup plan. We are called to spread the Good News of Jesus Christ and tell this world about His amazing love and grace. This world has its troubles, and it is full of sickness and heartache. Many people struggle with addictions, and we all have our own hurts, habits, and hang ups. Government programs are not the answer. Corporate America is not the solution, and Hollywood is surely not the answer. The Church is God's plan to change the world. God has placed all His stock in the Church.

In Luke 4:18-19 Jesus said, "The Spirit of the Lord is on me, because he has anointed me to preach the good news to the poor. He has sent me to proclaim freedom for the prisoners and recovery of sight for the blind, to release the oppressed, to proclaim the year of the Lord's favor."

That is what the Church is all about. That is the Father's business. It's not about having a cool church or having perfect attendance. It's about life change. Church, it's time to wake up. God has given us everything we need to get the job done. We have the power and authority through the Holy Spirit, and we have the message. Here is the good news. The Church of God will not be stopped. The Church of God will be victorious, and we will overcome. Don't forget that we are on the winning team.

Vision in the Church is cool. Strategy is needed and passion is exciting, but love is the fuel that will carry us through. We must translate His love to the world because they do not understand it. They do not understand it because they have never experienced it. I want the rest of the world to experience what God has given me. The Church is going forward. The Church will make a difference, and the Church of Jesus Christ will be victorious. "Father, open the doors of ministry and help us to step out on faith. Help us to trust you." God is still in the life changing business, and He wants to use you to do it.

Challenge for today: Answer these questions: What is your calling and purpose in life? What has God equipped you to do? What are you passionate about? What motivates you? Are you willing to be used by God? Are you walking in obedience and using the gifts that God has given you? He has called every believer to build His

Church, fulfill their purpose, and use their gifts for God's glory. What are you waiting for? Be the Church.

Praying Scripture

I encourage you to pray Psalm 119:33-40 to the Father today. Let it be your prayer to Him and wait around long enough to see what He says back to you. Psalm 119:33-40: "Teach me, O Lord, to follow your decrees; then I will keep them to the end. Give me understanding, and I will keep your law and obey it with all my heart. Direct me in the path of your commands, for there I find delight. Turn my heart towards your statutes and not towards selfish gains. Turn my eyes away from the worthless things: preserve my life according to your word. Fulfill your promise to your servant, so that you may be feared. Take away the disgrace I dread, for your laws are good. How I long for your precepts! Preserve my life in your righteousness." Amen.

Praying scripture is one of the most powerful things we can do as Christian believers. There is power in God's Word, and there is power in prayer. When we combine the two, lives will change, fears will crumble, strongholds will break down, and the world will stand amazed. "Lord, give us a hunger for your Word and a passion for prayer. Direct us and guide us in your ways, keep us, and preserve us like only you can." You will begin to hear from God when you use the Word of God in your prayers.

Challenge for today: Make a commitment to the Lord to become a student of the Word of God. Block out time in your week to study, memorize, and dive in deep to the Word. This must become a priority in your life. As you begin to follow through with your commitment to the Lord, find scripture that you can pray back to the Father. You can even pray it over a close friend or over yourself. This will be an investment that will come back to you tenfold. "Lord, give us understanding and wisdom that only You can give." May God bless you today.

Positioned

In this life, we usually don't get a position unless we can perform, and if we cannot keep up we often lose that position. That is not how it works in God's kingdom. In His kingdom, our position does not depend on our performance. Our position was purchased by Christ. The moment we welcomed Jesus in our life, our position changed from sinner to child of God. Nothing can change that. Nobody can ever take that away from us. Once we are in the family of God, we are living from a blessing.

Second Corinthians 5:17: "If anyone is in Christ, he is a new creation; the old is gone, the new has come!"

Colossians 3:3: "For you died, and now your life is hidden with Christ in God."

We are wrapped up in the Son of God. When God looks at us, He sees Christ. If we are hidden in Christ, quit getting lost in yourself. Jesus' performance has already secured our position in Him. Once we understand who we are, then we are free to do what we were redeemed to do.

Nothing or no one can pluck you from the Father's hands. Find rest in the security today that He has you in His hands. You do not have to impress Him. You are His.

Challenge for today: Commit Second Corinthians 5:17 to memory. Write it on a piece of paper and place it in your car, by the sink in the kitchen, or place it at your workstation in the office. Know that in Christ, you are a new creation, and you are a child of God. You have been made new by the blood of Jesus Christ. Take time to celebrate that good news and don't forget to shout it to the world.

Joint Adventure

Every farmer knows that unless he pursues his responsibilities to plow, plant, fertilize, and cultivate, he cannot expect a harvest at the end of the season. When you think about it, the farmer is in partnership with God. Farming is a joint venture between God and the farmer. The farmer cannot do what God must do, and God will not do what the farmer should do.

When it comes to holiness, this principle for a farmer is also true for us. The pursuit of holiness is a joint venture between God and every believer. No one can attain any degree of holiness without God working in his life. God has made it possible for us to walk in holiness. But He has given us the responsibility of walking it out. He doesn't do it for us. First Peter 1:15: "But just as he who called you is holy, so be holy in all you do; for it is written: Be holy, because I am holy."

The pursuit of holiness is not an option for a believer, but it is a partnership with Almighty God. God will do his part, now we must walk it out. The pursuit of holiness and becoming like Christ is a process and it will not happen overnight. There will be struggles and temptations that will stare us in the face, and there will be situations that will cause us to throw up our hands in frustration. Don't lose hope because we all struggle. God will give you everything you need to arrive at your destination. He will provide encouragement, energy, resources, and the people you need at just the right time. He is faithful, and He is in your corner. The God of the universe fights for us. This relationship and this adventure are about you and God walking hand in hand. "Help us to keep our eyes on You and trust in the promises of Your Word."

Challenge for today: What overwhelms you when we talk about holiness? Write down what comes to mind. Now, write out the word partnership and look up the definition of this word. Take time to think about the meaning, then write out your own definition of partnership. Spend time in prayer talking with your Father about your responsibilities. What are they? What is He calling you to do to grow in holiness? Then make a list of the things He has done to make this pursuit possible.

No Turning Back

Jesus spoke in Mark 8:34-36: "If anyone would come after me, he must deny himself and take up his cross and follow me. For whoever wants to save his life will lose it, but whoever loses his life for me and for the gospel will save it. What good is it for a man to gain the whole world, yet forfeit his soul?"

I have a simple thought that I want to share with you. No turning back. Rearview mirrors are very useful when it comes to driving but not living out life. Paul writes in Philippians 3:12-14: "Not that I have already obtained all this, or have already been made perfect, but I press on to take hold of that for which Christ Jesus took hold of me. Brothers, I do not consider myself yet to have taken hold of it. But one thing I do: Forgetting what is behind and straining toward what is ahead. I press on toward the goal to win the prize for which God has called me heavenward in Christ Jesus."

Paul knew what it was like to have a troubled past, and he knew the guilt that came along with those sins. Jesus changed everything. Because of his relationship with Jesus, he experienced forgiveness. Because of the grace of God, Paul didn't have to walk in shame and guilt. He didn't have to look back, but he could look forward.

If the world can be loud about sin, why can't the Church be loud about salvation and Jesus Christ? Following Jesus is not a fad or some happening tread; it's a calling. Jesus didn't come to establish a religion. He came to develop a personal relationship with you. Who is Jesus to you? If Jesus is Lord, He deserves more than our leftovers. He deserves our best; He deserves our worship. Don't run from suffering; embrace it. No turning back. Let go of guilt and shame. Keep moving forward and keep your eyes on Jesus. Take up your cross and follow Him.

Challenge for today: Is there a sin that haunts you? Is there guilt that keeps dragging you down? Are there regrets in your rearview mirror that you continue to look at again and again? Confess that to the Lord today. Be real and honest with Him and leave it there at His feet. Receive His mercy and grace. Then thank Him for His amazing grace and keep your eyes looking forward. No turning back.

Choose To Move Forward

Some people spend their whole life in regret - trying to overcome their past or the mistakes they have made. Trying to change the past is futile; and while you are looking back, it is hard to move forward. When a circus elephant is young, its trainer puts a chain around its ankle. This chain is tied to an anchor in the ground to keep the elephant from walking off. As the elephant gets older, bigger, and stronger, the trainer still uses the same chain and anchor which by now is not strong enough to hold this massive elephant. Yet, he will never try to escape because it is trained to believe that it can't break the chain. You see, it's not the chain holding the elephant back. It's the elephant's belief that holds it back. As a forgiven believer, you may believe that your past is holding you back, but the truth is, your past has no power over you.

Here is great news that comes from 1 John 1:8-9: "If we claim to be without sin, we deceive ourselves and the truth is not in us. If we confess our sins, he is faithful and just and will forgive us our sins and purify us from all unrighteousness."

What a powerful promise we have because of the blood of Christ. This is all because Jesus decided to take our place. He was willing to lay His life down on that old rugged cross. He was buried but three days later, He overcame sin and death, and now is sitting at the right hand of God. Our Jesus is alive and well. We have forgiveness because of His great love. In Romans 8:1-2 Paul tells us this, "Therefore, there is no condemnation for those who are in Christ Jesus, because through Christ Jesus the law of the Spirit of life set me free from the law of sin and death."

Experience the freedom that can only be found in Christ.

Challenge for today: Make a choice to walk in freedom. Take time to go to the altar of God and pour out your heart to Him and confess your sins. Ask Him to forgive you and cleanse you from guilt and shame. Thank Him for His amazing grace.

No Sin Too Big

Sin has touched us all. I don't care what you have done. If you will receive it, God's grace is more than enough. Romans 8:38-39: "For I am convinced that neither death nor life, neither angels nor demons, neither the present nor the future, nor any powers, neither height nor depth, nor anything else in all of creation, will be able to separate us from the love of God that is in Christ Jesus."

Thank you, Lord, for that promise.

We need to learn to look at Jesus and the cross instead of our sin. He doesn't condemn us, but He does convict us. Yes, there is a difference. Condemnation says you're heading down the wrong road and there is no turning around. Conviction says you are headed down the wrong road, but Jesus can help you turn around, and get on the right road. In 2 Corinthians 12:9 Paul tells us that Jesus said, "My grace is sufficient for you, for my power is made perfect in weakness. Therefore, I will boast all the more gladly about my weakness, so that Christ's power may rest on me."

Conviction is all about drawing us to Jesus.

Challenge for today: Thank You Lord for conviction, forgiveness, and a new life in Christ. Take a few minutes to thank Him for his goodness and provision. Then worship Him and give Him the glory He deserves.

He Did His Part

Start today out by praising God for His goodness, and then thank Him for three blessings in your life.

Hebrews 10:12-14: "But when this priest had offered for all time one sacrifice for sin, he sat down at the right hand of God. Since that time, he waits for his enemies to be made his footstool. For by one sacrifice, he was made perfect forever by those who are being made holy."

Jesus completed his job. He did not cower down or turn away. He made the walk up Golgotha for us. Jesus canceled our debt, and He nailed it to the cross. The penalty of sin has been paid for. Forgiveness has been offered. Sin is canceled. Our relationship with God has been restored. He did not die because of His own sin. He died because of my sin and yours. His precious blood was shed as the ultimate and final atonement for our sins. Jesus came to earth for a reason and a purpose. He came to die and give us freedom from the snares of sin.

In John 1:29, when John the Baptist saw Jesus, he shouted, "Look, the Lamb of God, who takes away the sins of the world."

One question remains. Have you received His work, His grace, His forgiveness, and the gift of eternal life? Say yes to Jesus today.

Challenge for today: Go back in time and reflect on your life when you received God's precious gift of grace through Jesus Christ. Take time to remember those people who were around you and the peace that filled your life. Now spend the next few minutes in a prayer thanking God for that day and for those who invested in you. Jesus didn't lose focus and didn't make excuses, but He fulfilled His purpose. What about you, are you fulfilling your purpose?

Overcomer

First John 5:4-5: "For everyone born of God overcomes the world. This is the victory that has overcome the world, even our faith. Who is it that overcomes the world? Only he who believes that Jesus is the Son of God."

The world will put labels on you, but God is in the business of changing your name. Throughout the Bible, God was changing names: "Abram" went from being childless to being "Abraham," the father of a nation. "Jacob" went from deceiver to "Israel," God's chosen people. "Simon" went from a frightened disciple to "Peter," whom Jesus called "the rock." "Saul" went from Christian-killer to "Paul," the greatest apostle ever.

Maybe you feel like you have no identity, or you think your sin is your identity. I believe that God has a new name for you and that your ability to receive it is limited only by your willingness to go to the Lord. In Christ, you can overcome the world. Place your faith in the One who has overcome sin and death. Victory is only found in Jesus. First John 5:12-13: "He who has the Son has life, he who does not have the Son of God does not have life. I write these things to you who believe in the name of the Son of God so that you may know that you have eternal life."

Church, we must spread this Good News everywhere we go. This world needs to hear the message of Jesus Christ. This world is not our home, we are just passing through, but we need to take as many as we can with us. He has overcome. "Thank you, Lord."

Challenge for today: Make a list of things you have overcome because of the love of Jesus Christ. I encourage you to be willing to share your story. Spread the Good News of Jesus with a close friend and don't put it off.

Plenty of Time?

The mighty eagle sat high on his perch. It was wintertime, and he spotted a dead carcass of a deer floating down a stream. Gliding from his perch, he landed on the dead deer, and began to eat. Then he heard the great waterfall just ahead. He said to himself, "I have plenty of time, I will eat and eat and just before the deer plunges over the edge. Then I will fly off." The waterfall got closer and closer. Getting to the very edge of the waterfall, the mighty eagle began to spread his wings and fly off. To his surprise, his claws had frozen solid to the deer carcass. He fell to his death that morning. What a costly meal.

If we don't consistently confess our sins to God, our sins will eventually destroy us. We need to learn to hate sin as God does. God loves the sinner but hates the sin. I want to encourage you with a few things.

1. Be teachable. Swallow pride and resist the thought of being indestructible. Live life with your spiritual eyes wide open. Don't allow pride to stand in your life.
2. Confession needs to be specific and don't hold to that sin. Give it to God right away.
3. Repent. Turn and run. Do a complete 180. How many times have we confessed our sins only to turn right back around and fall in the same trap?
4. Thank God for the gift of forgiveness. First John 1:9: "If we confess our sins, he is faithful and just and will forgive us our sins and purify us from all righteousness."

Challenge for today: Don't believe the lies of Satan. Sin is a big deal, and it will cause you so much pain and hurt. Sin is like cancer. If it is left alone, it will spread and grow, and it will start affecting other parts of your life. Take time to have a time of confession because we are not guaranteed tomorrow. Take care of your business with God now. Who knows when the waterfall is just ahead?

Some Things Don't Change

Pride, jealousy, and hatred have been in the human heart in all cultures, all the way back to Adam and Eve. They wanted to do things their own way which caused sin. Times haven't changed that much. Millions of people still want salvation, but on their own terms. They want to make their own way to God that works best for them. If Christianity is true, it's not a religion. Religion is man's effort to reach God. Religion can be anything. But Christianity is God coming to man in a personal relationship. I think we can all agree that man is instinctively religious, but God has chosen to reveal Himself to us through nature, scriptures, and through Jesus Christ.

First Peter 1:18-19: "For you know that it was not with perishable things such as silver or gold that you were redeemed from the empty way of life handed down to you from your forefathers, but with the precious blood of Christ, a lamb without blemish or defeat."

Jesus, the perfect Lamb of God, paid our debt. He took our place and gave us life. That is the Good News today. Let's celebrate this with every step we take and take time to give thanks for His wonderful grace. It's all about the relationship.

Challenge for today: Evaluate your relationship with God. How would you describe your walk with God? Is it growing or is it just existing? Take steps to freshen up that relationship with Him. Plug in some worship music, turn it up, and worship. Take time to listen to His voice; He wants to speak to you.

Let It Sink In

For those of us that spend time grilling, the meat is always better when you marinate it. Thaw the meat the day before and create your marinade. Place the meat in the marinade overnight, and what happens? The flavor soaks into the meat through and through. Paul writes in First Corinthians 15:9-10: "For I am the least of the apostles and do not deserve to be called an apostle because I persecuted the church of God. But by the grace of God, I am what I am, and his grace to me was not without effect. No, I worked harder than all of them-yet not I, but the grace of God that was in me."

It is only by the grace of God that we can be called a child of God, spiritually alive, heavenly positioned, connected to God, a billboard of mercy, and an honored child. Let that sink in. Let it marinate. How much better to begin your day thinking victory and not defeat? Awake to grace this morning and not shame.

How many times are we guilty of dwelling on the negative and focusing on the things we do not have in this life? How much time do we spend complaining and whining about things that we have no control over? Remind yourself what a pleasure it is to be called a Child of God. It is all because of the grace of God. Let that truly soak in and offer Him some praise.

Challenge for today: I challenge you to profess three things out loud:
First, profess that you are a child of God.
Second, profess that this day you will live for the glory of God.
Lastly, profess out loud that sin has no authority over you any longer.

Come thirsty. Receive His work, and let grace run deep. Living the Christian life is not about a list of do's and don'ts. It is all about an intimate relationship with a Holy God. Thank Him for His amazing grace.

Let Grace Go Deep

What good is water if you don't drink? What good is grace if you don't let it go deep? How would you describe your heart today? Do you see your heart as a water drenched kid in front of an opened fire hydrant or as a dried-up desert tumbleweed? It's all about God's grace.

Ephesians 2:4-9: "But because of his great love for us, God, who is rich in mercy, made us alive with Christ even when we were dead in our transgressions-it is by grace you have been saved. And God raised us up with Christ and seated us with him in the heavenly realms in Christ Jesus. In order that in the coming ages he might show the incomparable riches of his grace, expressed in his kindness to us in Christ Jesus. For it is by grace you have been saved, through faith-and this not from yourselves, it is the gift of God-not of works, so that no one could boast. For we are God's workmanship, created in Christ Jesus to do good works, which God prepares in advance for us to do."

Grace is more than just a blessing prayed over a meal. When someone graces us with their presence, we feel honored that they showed up. When we say a ballerina is graceful, she is light on her toes and flows easily with much beauty. God's gracious gift of salvation is a very undeserved gift unlike any other. If I show up at my wife's job with flowers on our anniversary, she will think she deserved them for putting up with me for all those years. However, if I showed up with flowers on any given Wednesday morning for no reason, she might be blown away with my gift. She would wonder what I had done wrong or what she had done to get them.

God's grace is BIG. God's grace defines us. Grace is the reason we can have a relationship with our Heavenly Father because we certainly do not deserve His time and attention. We should be on our knees daily thanking God for giving us grace and mercy. His forgiveness and compassion are undeserving, but also unconditional. He shows up for us every day, and we have done nothing to warrant it.

Challenge for today: Define grace. What does it mean to you and how does it change your life? The simplest way to define grace is by describing it as: God's riches at Christ's expense. You have received grace; now how do you give grace away? Surely there is someone you know who needs this precious gift.

What Are You Harvesting?

I just moved out to the country, right in the middle of a farming community. I have always lived in a neighborhood close to the city. Things are a little different here, but it is really growing on me. I have seen more tractors, combines, and farm equipment in the last six months than I have ever seen in my entire life. I have a field right here in my backyard. There is a lot of work and expense that goes on especially getting the fields prepared for planting. Then comes the planting, irrigating and the months of caring for the crop. Next comes the harvest, a time when you bring in all the crops from the fields. Jesus said in John 4:35, "I tell you, open your eyes and look at the fields! They are ripe for harvest."

We must do our part and we must be found faithful.

James 3:17-18: "But the wisdom that comes from heaven is first of all pure; then peace-loving, considerate, submissive, full of mercy and good fruit, impartial and sincere. Peacemakers who sow in peace raise a harvest of righteousness."

Stop and ask yourself, "What does this mean to me?" What am I harvesting? Am I putting in the work? I encourage you to walk in the presence of the Lord. Receive from the Lord and fill up on his love, mercy, grace, and goodness. As you fill up on God's goodness, think of ways to replant his love all over this world. Preparation is so important when it comes to a great harvest. Yes, it will take a lot of blood, sweat, and tears to plant spiritual seeds in this world, and it will not happen overnight. Know this, God is faithful, and He will do His part. Invest in things that will last forever - the souls of mankind.

Challenge for today: Ask the Lord to open your mind and your heart to the possibilities. We must throw out the seed if we want a harvest.

Line Up with God

God created people to enjoy the good things he made, even after Adam and Eve sinned. The problem comes when we start worshiping those created things instead of the Creator. Worshiping the created will always lead to disappointment. First John 2:15-17: "Don't love the world or anything in the world. If anyone loves the world, the love of the Father is not in him. For everything in the world-the cravings of the sinful man, the lust of his eyes and the boasting of what he has and does not have, comes not from the Father but from the world. The world and its desires pass away, but the man who does the will of God lives forever."

The world does not see beyond today. It's all about the moment. The world can deliver success, power, and pleasure, but it will never be enough. Chasing the things of this world will leave you empty and eventually falling into sin. Sin will always take us further than we want to go, and it keeps us there longer than we want to stay. What are you investing in? Building a life in the world will leave you bankrupt and very disappointed.

Challenge for today: I encourage you to give God first place. Stop pursuing the things of this world and build your house on the Rock. It's so easy to get off track and get sideswiped by debt, wanting more and more. Before you know it, you are way over your head trying just to survive your monthly bills. Pray this prayer: "God take over. I give you the control of my heart." Take time to worship the King and give Him all the glory today.

Can You Imagine?

What if there was a big screen available for all to see, and your sins were broadcast on the screen? Can you imagine what it would be like if people knew you by the sins you have committed. In other words, your sins would become your identity. That would be terrible. No one I know would walk up and identify themselves as a "Liar" or "Cheat" or "Fraud." We would be crazy to do that to ourselves, but we will surely do it to other people. We would never hang those labels around our necks for all to see, so why do we do it to others?

So many people wear masks at church because they are too afraid to show their true selves for fear of being judged or condemned. Think about it. Apostle Paul would have a hard time being a pastor in today's Church. He couldn't get past the background check because he was a murderer. It is so easy to place labels on other people, and we all are guilty. As far as I know, there has only been one perfect person to ever walk the face of this earth, and His name was Jesus. Be willing to show grace and take time to look for the good in other people. Romans 5:8: "But God demonstrates his own love for us in this: While we were still sinners, Christ died for us."

He overlooked my imperfections. Shouldn't we do the same for those around us? We often want to expose others to make ourselves feel better. We have all sinned; it's time to be real.

Challenge of today: Drop the mask that you tend to wear. Put off all pretense and get real with the Father. Know that you are dearly loved by God and His grace is more than enough. Let Him have His way with you and surrender your entire being to His will.

The Deadly Disease

There is a disease that no culture can avoid. There is a disease that no nation can escape. There is a disease no person can sidestep. It's called sin. Adam and Eve turned their faces toward the hissing snake; and for the first time - they ignored God. Eve didn't ask God what to do when Satan tempted her. Adam didn't suggest, "Let's consult the Creator." They acted as if they had no Heavenly Father. Sin entered the world. Sin sees the world with no God in it, where we see sin as a slip up. But God sees sin as a godless attitude that leads to godless actions.

Isaiah 53:6: "We all, like sheep, have gone astray, each of us has turned to his own way."

The sinful mind dismisses God. We allow His counsel to fall to the wayside. His plan, unconsidered. What happens is the lack of God-centeredness leads to self-centeredness. God says to love, and we choose to hate. God instructs us to forgive, and we opt to get even. Sin for a season will quench that thirst, but it will leave you empty and thirsty. Romans 6:8: "Those controlled by the sinful nature cannot please God."

God has made it clear through scripture that the plague of sin will not cross His shores of Heaven. The infected soul will never walk the streets of gold. But there is good news. Sin may entice you, but it will not enslave you. It will touch you, discourage you, or distract you, but it cannot condemn you. This is for those who are in Christ Jesus. Romans 8:1: "There is now no condemnation for those who are in Christ Jesus."

We have been set free by the blood of Jesus Christ. I urge you to trust in this truth. Trust the work of God for you and trust the presence of Christ in you. In Christ, we are not fatally afflicted by sin, so don't live as though we are. We are forgiven. Sin may touch us, but it cannot claim us. Christ in me, the Hope of Glory. Trust His work for you.

Challenge for today: This is going to be a strange challenge. For the next seven hours set an alarm at the top of each hour. When the alarm goes off, stop what you are doing, and thank God for the gift of salvation. Pour out a heart of gratitude for His amazing grace, and His love.

God Is for You

Psalm 139:5: "You hem me in behind and before, and you lay your hand upon me."

I wanted to share a simple message with you today, "God is for you." He protects you and He has a crazy, good plan for your life. He has a purpose for you in His kingdom. He has surrounded you and has placed His hand on you. When this Psalm was written, it was an accepted practice that when someone "blessed" another person, he laid his hand upon the person he blessed.

There are a lot of things I could do without during this lifetime. I could survive without ESPN; it's not a must. I don't have to have a lot of money, and I sure don't want to climb the corporate ladder to gain power, or position. But I can't do without God's hand on my life. I need His blessing and favor.

Romans 8:31: "If God is for us, who can be against us?"

Isaiah 54:17: "No weapon formed against us will prosper."

Romans 8:37: "We are more than conquerors through him that loved us."

We all know too well that our enemies will rise-up, people will stab us in the back, and so-called friends will try to put us down. But if God is for us, who can be against us? "Thank you, Lord."

Challenge for today: I encourage you to say these verses out loud throughout the day. Run them through your mind repeatedly. Know that God's hand of favor is on you, and you are a child of the living King. Never forget that you and God make a majority.

He Loves You

Let's start our day off right in Psalms. Psalm 139:1-4: "O Lord, you have searched me and you know me. You know when I sit and when I rise; you perceive my thoughts from afar. You discern my going out and my lying down; you are familiar with all my ways. Before a word is on my tongue you know it completely, O Lord."

He knows me in such an intimate way, and He even knows the dark corners of my heart, but He still loves me. It is not just that God knows me, but He watches me, and He cherishes me.

Have you ever tried to have a conversation with someone who seemed distracted? You know that person who is talking with you but will not take his eyes off the T.V.? How about the guy who looks past you, and is looking for the next person to connect with? We all know that person who can't wait till you get finished talking to be able to tell you what they think. It can be frustrating because they are not focusing on you, and it seems as if they don't care. That is not God. He is never in a rush because He has all eternity, and I believe He enjoys one-on-one conversations with us.

I remember watching my girls sleep when they were babies. I remember seeing them breathe and move around, and they were so adorable. They were always dressed to a "T" when it was bedtime. I treasure those memories, and I will never forget them. Our Heavenly Father isn't preoccupied with something else. He even watches us sleep, and He cares about the smallest details of our lives. You are loved, adored, and cherished by the King. Let's celebrate this truth today.

Challenge for today: Say this out loud, "I am loved by God." Be reassured that He cares for you, and He always has your back. Our Heavenly Father never sleeps or slumbers, and He is always watching over us even when we don't know it.

Being Shaped

Jeremiah 18:1-4: "This is the word that came to Jeremiah from the Lord: 'Go down to the potter's house, and there I will give you my message.' So I went down to the potter's house, and I saw him working at the wheel. But the pot he was shaping from the clay was marred in his hands; so the potter formed it into another pot, shaping it as it seemed best to him."

We all have been shaped by our experiences in life, most of which were beyond our control. God allowed them for His purpose of molding you. We all have faced hurts, trials, and difficult times. Some more than others, but know this: God never wastes a hurt. I believe God intentionally allows you to go through painful experiences to equip you for ministry. It is a time of preparation. Second Corinthians 1:4: "He comforts us in all our troubles so that we can comfort others. When others are troubled, we will be able to give them the same comfort God has given us."

We will never know all the answers to our questions when it comes to this life, but know that God is good. He is at His wheel shaping and molding you in love. I encourage you not to hide your pain, but to share your pain. Tell others how God's grace has helped you in your weakness and see how the doors of ministry will fling open.

Challenge for today: Keep your head up, keep moving forward, and keep your eyes on Christ. Know that you are loved by the God of all creation, and He has your back. He is always working behind the scenes.

Where Are You Going in Such a Rush?

Philippians 1:6: "Be confident of this, that he who began a good work in you will carry it on to completion until the day of Jesus Christ."

One of life's frustrations is that God's timetable is rarely the same as ours. God is never in a hurry, but he is always on time. He will use your entire lifetime to prepare you for your role for eternity. Look at the life of Moses. God took 80 years to prepare Moses; 40 of those years were in the desert. I don't know about you, but I am a very impatient person. I am like that kid in the back seat of the car that is headed on a long trip. You know that kid, that kid that keeps asking, "Are we there yet? How much farther?" But God is patient, and He will never rush the process. You can count on that.

When God wants to make a mushroom, he does it overnight, but when He wants to make an oak tree, He takes 100 years. Slow down, be patient, and wait on the Lord. God doesn't need your help; He is quite capable of working everything out.

I have been known to put things together without using the instructions because in my mind, reading the instructions will take too long. So, I spread out all the pieces, looked at the box, and I started putting everything together. Somehow, there always seems to be leftover parts. Most of the time, I end up taking something back apart. Finally, I slow down enough to read the instructions which seems to work a whole lot better.

Challenge for today: Be patient and willing to wait for God. There are no shortcuts when it comes to maturity. Believe God is working in your life even when you don't feel it. Even the snail made it to the ark, eventually.

Difficult Times

Without faith it's impossible to please God. Why? Because faith and trust must merge from love. Are you willing to ask God a difficult question? More importantly, are you willing to listen to God's answer? Raising kids is a never-ending task, to say the least. Let me tell you, it's a journey. Life is full of mountain tops and valleys. So many of us want to believe in God's presence and goodness, but sometimes we have so many questions. We long to trust Him, to feel His presence, to sink into His peace, to believe He is there for us, and that He will carry our burdens. We want to know that He hears us and that He will protect us. I know there are a lot of people who once believed that God took an active interest in their lives, but now they are not so sure.

Do you ever question God? Especially during those difficult times, those times when nothing makes sense, or nothing seems to be going your way. You are not alone. Throughout life, we all reach a point where we find ourselves wrestling with spiritual questions about grief, anger, and temptation. The enemy will use anything to put distance between you and God. When we are going through these difficult times and stumbling in the valleys of life, it is difficult to see the good. You want to believe in God's goodness. There will be times in our lives when we doubt whether God sees our pain and sometimes, we wonder if God even cares. If you are struggling today, I'm hoping you are willing to wrestle. Just remember, God didn't say life would be easy, but He did tell us that He will never leave us or forsake us. To really know God, you must wrestle through pain, suffering, doubt, and unanswered questions. If you wrestle with God, run after Him. Stay by His side, and God will meet you in your pain. David wrote Psalm 6:2-3: "Be merciful to me, Lord, for I am faint; O Lord, heal me, for my bones are in agony. My soul is in anguish. How long, O Lord, how long?"

Can you relate to David's pain? He was exhausted, worn out, depressed, and alone. He had cried many tears and David simply couldn't understand why the God who has the power to change his circumstance, would not do it. Think about it: If we understood everything completely, we wouldn't need faith, would we?

Challenge for today: Be willing to wrestle with God and to ask Him those difficult questions. Be willing to sit still and listen to what He has to say back to you. Don't get in a hurry.

A Mere Shadow or An Echo?

Colossians 1:15-18: "He is the image of the invisible God, the firstborn over all creation. For by Him all things were created: things in heaven and on earth, visible and invisible, whether thrones or powers or rulers or authorities; all things were created by him and for him. He is before all things, and in him all things hold together. And he is the head of the body, the church; he is the beginning and the firstborn from among the dead, so that in everything he might have supremacy."

God is the only given in the universe. He always has and He always will be. Everything else comes and goes, but Jesus Christ is what holds it all together. We were created to enjoy and display the Creator's glory.

First Corinthians 6:19-20: "Do you not know that your body is a temple of the Holy Spirit, who is in you, whom you have received from God? You are not your own; you were bought with a price. Therefore, honor God with your body."

We exist to display the glory of God. When we fulfill this reason for being, we have substance, meaning, and purpose. When we don't fulfill this purpose in our life, we are a mere shadow of what God has for us. God has not made us to be mere shadows and echoes. We were made to have a God-like substance. We were made to make God-like music. We were made to have a God-like impact on this world. When I forsake my God and I love other things more, I become like the things I love, small and insignificant. We need to break away from small thinking and worldly desires. We are called to set our face to God and get to know Him, enjoy Him, and to live for Him. Will we wake up from the slumbers of shadowland existence? What will we leave behind? Will it be a mere shadow or an echo? Will it be a tribute on earth and written down in heaven forever?

Challenge for today: Pray: "Father, forgive me for wasting so much time. Forgive me for my love affair with empty things. Show Yourself to us in your fullness. Wake us up to the life You want for us." Live life with no regrets. The time is now.

The Noise of Our Culture

Jim was a grocery store clerk, and he loved his job. He was a hard worker, and he was very intentional with his customers. Jim's one pet peeve was out of control toddlers and parents who yelled at their kids but did nothing about it. One evening, Jim was checking out a customer who had a shopping cart full of groceries. While ringing up the sale, a child behind him began screaming loudly, and an angry man responded by shouting, "Get down!" Jim thought, "What a jerk," without even looking up. He kept calling out prices and moving the groceries past the scanner. The kid was still crying and again the man yelled, "Get down!" Talking about poor parenting, this guy was a total jerk. Jim kept on checking groceries out without looking up. Finally, he finished, and Jim looked up and said, "That will be $89.95." Seeing no one, he looked around and noticed everyone, including his customers, lying face down on the floor. He turned around just in time to see the gunman running out of the store. The clerk behind him, still on the floor, said, "Jim, you know the second time you heard get down, his gun was pointed at your head." We get so accustomed to the noise of our culture, and the distraction of the world that when we hear something important, we blow it off as if it were insignificant.

Second Corinthians 6:2: "I tell you, now is the time of God's favor, now is the day of salvation." Take time to look up. Who or what has your attention today? What is the passion of your heart?

Challenge for today: Be sensitive to the voice of God in your life. I know how hard it can be with so much going on in our world, but it's an investment that will pay off in the long run.

For His Pleasure

Why do you exist? I challenge you today to stop long enough to answer this question. What is your response?

We exist for His benefit, His glory, His purpose, and His delight. Bringing pleasure to God is called worship. Anything you do that brings pleasure to God is an act of worship. If we fail to worship God, we will always find a substitute. Many people think of worship as songs we sing at church, but worship is far more than this. Worship is a lifestyle. Every activity can be transformed into an act of worship when we do it for the praise, glory, and pleasure of God. We all have our music style that we like best, but our music style says more about us than it says about God. When we worship, our goal is to bring pleasure to God, not ourselves.

If you ever said, "I didn't get anything out of worship today," you worshiped for the wrong reason. I am so guilty. Worship isn't for you. It's for God. Our purpose is to bring glory and honor to our Creator. Isaiah 29:13: the Lord says: "These people come near to me with their mouths and honor me with their lips, but their hearts are far from me. Their worship of me is made of only rules taught by men."

The people were offering fancy, meaningless, and empty words. They were just going through the motions of man-made rituals. Have you ever been there?

How can we do everything to the glory of God? Answer: By doing everything as if you were doing it for Jesus. Even your work can become your worship if you dedicate it to God and perform it with an awareness of His presence. Yes, even cleaning out my gutters can be a form of worship today.

Challenge for today: Be aware of His presence and worship the King. Enjoy His presence. Is your life bringing Him pleasure?

Cleaning Out the Gutters

Out of all the houses I have bought over the years, I only had one house that had gutters. It may be the only house I ever have with gutters. They are so difficult to clean out, especially during the Fall. Leaves and pine straw fall from the trees straight into the gutters. I understand it helps direct the water flow from the roof, and it works great when the gutters are free of pine straw and leaves. I am guilty of not cleaning them out as I should, and I have allowed them to get out of hand. Now the water flow is restricted, and my gutters are not directing the water to the proper areas. I have been putting this task off for some time, and I have used every excuse under the sun not to get it done. No more excuses. I will free my gutters and let the water flow once again. I will get it done.

What about your spiritual gutters? Have trash and other things clogged them up? Has the spiritual flow been restricted? Have we been so busy with everything else that we have neglected what really needs to be handled? Too many times we allow sin to hang on to our hearts, and we put off doing anything about it. Let today be the day you get it done and stop making excuses for neglecting your spiritual gutters. David knew what it was like to have his spiritual gutter full of trash, and his water flow all clogged up. He was miserable and desperate, so he cried out to the Lord for help. Hear his cry in Psalm 51:1-2, "Have mercy on me, O God, according to your unfailing love; according to your great compassion, blot out my transgressions (clean out my gutters). Wash away all my iniquities and cleanse me from my sin."

Psalm 51:10-12: "Create in me a pure heart, O God, and renew a steadfast spirit within me. Don't cast me from your presence or take your Holy Spirit from me. Restore to me the joy of my salvation."

David used a prayer of forgiveness to clean out his spiritual gutters and it allowed his spirit flow to move again. His joy was restored.

Challenge for today: Today is the day. Get before the Lord, and get it done. Start by confessing your sins.

What Matters Most

O ne of my greatest passions in life is to share God's Word and to make it fun to understand God's truths. I know the difference that Jesus can make in one's life. My heart is to see others come to a saving knowledge of knowing Jesus, growing in that relationship, and then sharing it with the world. Lord, "equip me to do your work, and let your name be glorified because of it."

First Corinthians 13:3: "No matter what I say, what I believe, and what I do, I am bankrupt without love."

Second John 1:6: "Love means living the way God commanded us to live. As you have heard from the beginning, his command is this; Live a life of love."

Because God is love, the most important lesson, the one thing He wants us to learn here on earth, is how to love. It is in loving that we are most like Him. Learning to love unselfishly is not always easy. He wants His family to be known for its love more than anything else. But know this, busyness is one of the greatest enemies of building relationships and loving others. It's so easy to get preoccupied with making a living, paying bills, and doing life. The point of life is learning to love God and the people around you. Love lasts forever. Love leaves a legacy. Mother Teresa said, "It's not what you do, but how much love you put into it that matters."

Challenge for today: Ask the Lord what you need to do to grow in His love. Then take time to look around you and slow down long enough to see those who are in desperate need. Make yourself available to be used by God. It is time to make a difference.

Quiet Worship/Noisy Gratitude

I hope you are having a good week. Psalm 95:1-3; 6-7: "Come, let us sing for joy to the Lord; let us shout aloud to the Rock of our salvation. Let us come before him with thanksgiving and extol him with music and song. For the Lord is the great God, the great King above all gods. Come let us bow down in worship, let us kneel before the Lord our Maker; for He is our God, and we are the people of His pasture, and the flock under His care."

I went to work out last week, and I always get started with cardio. So, I went over to some machines and began my workout. As I said hello to a couple of my buddies, I noticed this one lady walking on the treadmill. She had her ear buds in, and you could tell she was enjoying her music as she worked out. She was getting energized by her music, and she was smiling from ear to ear. About 10 minutes later, she broke out in song. With a loud voice, she was praising Jesus right there in the middle of the gym. She got lost in the moment, and she was so full of Jesus, she had to let it out. I loved it. Our quiet worship should turn into noisy gratitude. We were dead, but now we are alive. Let's not continue acting as if we are dead.

Psalm 100:1-4: "Shout for joy to the Lord, all the earth. Worship the Lord with gladness; come before him with joyful songs. Know that the Lord is God. It is he who made us, and we are his; we are his people, the sheep of his pasture. Enter his gates with thanksgiving and his courts with praise; give thanks to him and praise his name."

Raise the roof with thanksgiving and praise.

Challenge for today: Take time to worship Him and allow His love to fill you to a point of overflowing. Then express your gratitude and thankfulness to the Father loudly. It will do you some good.

Take Over

Ephesians 2:4-5: "But because of his great love for us, God, who is rich in mercy, made us alive with Christ even when we were dead in transgressions-It was by grace you have been saved."

Jesus didn't come to sit on an earthly throne or win a popularity contest. He didn't come to earth for a makeover. He came for a takeover. He came to defeat sin and death once and for all. Jesus is so much more than just a good teacher and a great example to follow. He is the King of kings and the Lord of lords! He is the Savior of the world. He showed us incredible grace that day he died on that rugged cross. Even though we didn't deserve it, He willingly took our place, and He took the sting of death. That is the greatest picture of love, mercy, and grace.

Ephesians 2:7-8: "For it was by grace you have been saved, through faith-and this not from yourselves, it is a gift of God, not of works, so that no one can boast."

Jesus pursued us when we had nothing to offer in return. In our sin and shame Jesus died for us. What a display of grace. Jesus is in the business of resurrecting, redeeming, and restoring. Stop running from the One who loves you the most. You are never too far gone that His grace can't redeem you and restore you. The bigger the mess, the greater the grace.

Challenge for today: How has God shown you grace? Take time to praise Him for that grace. Thank Jesus for laying down His life on that old rugged cross. Thank Him for overcoming sin and death when He came out of that tomb.

Oh, How We Forget

As a child, I remember singing a chorus that said, "He's got the whole world in His hands." I loved singing that song and doing all the hand motions with my friends at church. We would get to stand before the whole church on Sunday night and sing a couple of songs. It was called "Little Folks Choir." We always brought the house down. We must have been great singers or just cute kids, because they always clapped.

But if we believe God has the whole world in His hands, and He is in total control, why do we worry so much? If He has everything in control, surely, He can take care of us. In Matthew 6:25-27 Jesus said, "Therefore I tell you, do not worry about your life, what you will eat or drink; or about your body, what you will wear. Isn't life more important than food, and the body more important than clothes? Look at the birds of the air, they do not sow or reap or store away in barns, and yet the Heavenly Father feeds them. Are you not much more valuable than they are? Who are you worried can add a single hour to your life?"

If His eye is on the sparrow, He will surely watch over you. He is about to raise a beautiful sunrise just to see you smile. He is working for you without you even asking. That is real love. God didn't have to make the sun rise this morning, and He didn't have to give us His Son. But He did. Thank Him for His amazing love, and always going the extra mile to display it. Lay worry aside, and trust in His goodness.

Challenge for today: What are you worrying about? Take that load off your shoulder and give it to the God of the universe. Leave it there with Him and take time to thank Him. Know this, He cares for you. All day, every day.

Holding Pattern?

Have you ever felt like your life is in a holding pattern? There is a ton of stuff going on around you, but you're not really going anywhere. And your soul is wanting more. Do you ever grow tired of the status quo, and long for something more fulfilling? I believe our restlessness is a holy discontentment. In fact, it is likely that God has made you restless. He may be stirring up a hunger for a powerful work He is about to bring in your life. He wants you so hungry for His "more" that you will pursue it. The ones who feel spiritually full and satisfied may never taste "the more" that God has for them.

As a child, I loved playing sports, and I treasured all my trophies that I received. I hung them on the wall and reorganized them every time I received a new one. As I grew older, I still loved to get trophies, but they came in different shapes and forms. My trophies became a bigger house, more money, and promotions at work. You guessed it, all this stuff will leave you empty and longing for more. Those trophies that meant so much to me are in a dump somewhere covered up with garbage. Give me more, something that matters; something that will last forever.

Do you ever have a stirring inside of you that is telling you: I want to make a greater difference with the rest of my life than I have made until now? God loves taking an ordinary Joe from his small world to a life bigger than he could ever dream. God is still in the life enlargement business. "God, blow the lid off my safe life, and let it count for your glory. Take this hunger, discontentment, restlessness, and passion and impact the lives of people around me. Here I am Lord."

Challenge for today: Identify your holy discontentment. What is God stirring up inside of you? Tell God you are willing to do whatever He calls you to do.

Encouragement

I want to give you a spoon full of encouragement. Sometimes we find ourselves dragging at the end of our work week. We have so many things going on, and we have our hands in so many different things. I encourage you to get recharged by spending time with the Creator of the universe. Turn on your favorite worship music, close your eyes, and see the face of Jesus. Take time to praise Him for all the blessings in your life. Stop thinking about all the negative things around you and thank Him for His amazing love and mercy. Open His love letter to you, and receive all the goodness He has for you, as a child of God. Worship Him and be full of the Holy Spirit. Let His love rise-up, and fill you to a point of overflowing, so that He will get on everything you touch. Don't let your tank run empty.

Hebrews 13:5: "Keep your lives free from the love of money and be content with what you have, because God has said, 'Never will I leave you; never will I forsake you.'"

He is faithful. The things of the world will pass away and will leave you empty. Hebrews 13:8: "Christ is the same yesterday, today, and forever."

My God is good, and He is good all the time. Face today with great courage, get recharged by the unchanged God, and let others see the difference He can make in their lives. "Yes Lord."

Challenge for today: Spend extra time in God's Word and just soak in His presence. Turn your focus on Him and push all other cares aside. I challenge you to turn your phone off for an hour. Praise Him because He is worthy of praise.

Experience True Love

First Corinthians 13:4-7: "Love is patient, love is kind. It does not envy, it doesn't boast, it is not proud. It does not dishonor others, it is not self-seeking, it is not easily angered, it keeps no record of wrongs. Love does not delight in evil but rejoices in truth. It always protects, always trusts, always hopes, always perseveres."

We are loved by God with an Agape type of love. Agape love is all about action. It has nothing to do with feelings, and it has nothing to do with whether the other person deserves it. Agape love forgives, and it never quits.

It's sad to see how many people who have a deep longing for love, without any idea of where they can find the type of love they need. We all need to be loved unconditionally, and there is only one person who can love us like that, Jesus Christ. Jesus doesn't just love us because He feels like it. He loves us because we need agape love. He created us that way. His love is so great and ever present that I often take His love for granted. True love is found in a personal love relationship with Jesus Christ. Take time to thank the Father for His amazing love, and for sending His very best to bridge the gap. Have an awesome day, and don't forget to kick a dent in the gates of Hell.

Challenge for today: List three ways God has shown you love in your past. Give Him some praise and celebrate that amazing love.

Don't Want Sympathy, But Compassion Is Needed

Never take a day for granted or wish it away. Learn to enjoy the ups and the downs of life. What would roller coasters be without them? Enjoy the ride and take time to smile. I want to share a quick thought with you today.

Luke 7:13 says that Jesus "had compassion" on the widow. Compassion means to have a feeling of sorrow followed by a deep desire to alleviate suffering. Knowing this, Jesus sees our pain and experiences our suffering and has a deep desire to alleviate that suffering. Most of us experience sympathy when we see others go through hard times or face difficult situations. It usually doesn't lead us to do much to alleviate the suffering. The difference between sympathy and compassion is action. Jesus reaches out to the widow, and He does something about it. He brought her son back to life. Jesus loves us in such a way that we can't even comprehend. He cares how we feel. If we experience sorrow, He feels it too.

People don't need our sympathy, but I guarantee you they need our compassion. Love others the way Christ loves us. When our eyes are so focused on ourselves, we will never see the needs of people around us. Look into the eyes of Christ and see the reflection of what He is looking at. Then do something about it.

Challenge of today: Examine your heart and motives and spend time in prayer talking with the Father about your life. Ask God to keep your heart in check and give you a spirit of compassion. Open your spiritual eyes and see the needs of people around you. Be willing to step out of your comfort zone to love on people.

Don't Cry

Luke 7:11-13: "Jesus went to a town called Nain, and his disciples and a large crowd went along with him. As he approached the town gate, a dead person was being carried out-the only son of his mother, and she was a widow. And a large crowd from town was with her. When the Lord saw her, his heart went out to her and he said, 'Don't Cry.'"

Can you imagine what God's timing for the widow in this story must have been like. This poor widow had lost her husband and now her only son. She was hurting and she had to be overwhelmed. As their paths crossed, Jesus said to the widow, "Don't cry." Do what? "Don't cry? Did Jesus realize what she had just experienced? Can't you see that my only son is dead? But Jesus didn't say don't cry to offend her, but to give her hope. Jesus was about to teach us that God is never late. His timing is perfect. Jesus walked over to the coffin and said to the son, "Get up." Luke 7:15: "The dead man sat up and began to talk, and Jesus gave him back to his mother."   Can you imagine that union?

God is never late. You may feel like you are in a hopeless situation, and you feel overwhelmed. You may be experiencing frustration, and you feel like your prayers are not being answered. Know this, if God can answer a widow's prayer to heal her son, he can give you exactly what you need at exactly the right time. It may not be right now, but at the right time. Hang in there.

Challenge of today: Tell God what is on your mind. Life can be so overwhelming and can deflate your spirit in a furry. There will be things that will knock us down and beat us up, but we have a God who loves us enough to say, "Get up." Trust God with your circumstance and believe He is standing at your side. Lean on Him and He will help you to walk through this difficult time.

At Just the Right Time

Romans 5:6: "You see, at just the right time, when we were still powerless, Christ died for the ungodly."

At our lowest moment, he did his greatest work. He came for us at just the right time. Timing is everything, and our job is to learn to trust God's timing even when we would rather have our desires met right now. That is so hard to do because we are so impatient. For us, it is hard to wait on a hamburger at a drive through window, much less waiting on God to answer our prayers about a huge burden in life.

Romans 8:28: "In all things God works for the good of those who love Him, who have been called according to his purpose."

In all things. All circumstances. All events. All frustrations. All trials. All defeats. For believers, this means that when you did not get what you wanted when you wanted it, it's because God knew that there was something better for you. God is looking out for your good. Just know that God has your back. In His timing, at just the right time, He will reveal all truth to you in your time of need. Bank on it.

Challenge for today: Are you impatient? Are you trying to run ahead of God? Then stop, slow down, take a time out, and sit with the Father. Don't even say a word. Just enjoy His presence in a time of hurt, pain, and suffering. Take time to rest your mind, body, and your spirit. Then confess your doubts, worries, and your stress. Then renew your trust and faith in Him to handle every situation in your life. He is big enough to handle every situation.

Come Thirsty My Friend

John 7:37-38: "On the last and greatest day of the Feast, Jesus stood and said in a loud voice, 'If anyone is thirsty, let him come to me and drink. Whoever believes in me, as the Scripture has said, streams of living water will flow from within you.'"

Deprive your body of the necessary fluids and see what warning signs go off in you. Our eyes need water to cry. Our mouth needs moisture to swallow, and our glands need sweat to keep our body cool. Our body needs water the same way a tire needs air. For the human body, it is so important to stay hydrated.

Recently, my wife's car engine light came on. That is never a good sign. This engine light is designed to come on to let us know that something isn't just right with the car's performance. It gives us a heads up to get the engine checked out before you are left beside the road. How many times do we ignore the warning signs that God tries to give us letting us know that something is off, and that we need to pay more attention to it? Sometimes we are so deep into life that we just don't have time to slow down. Even when the warning lights are flashing in our face.

What water can do for your body; Jesus can do for the heart. Are you tired and worn out? Do waves of worry, fear, guilt, and loneliness overwhelm you at times? Jesus can soften the hardest heart and hydrate what is dry. Do you need a drink from a well that does not run dry? Allow Jesus to take over and kick 'self' off the throne. Receive His love and mercy. We don't have to live this life with a dehydrated heart. Jesus has given us an open invitation to come and drink. You must be willing to receive it. Come thirsty, my friend.

Challenge for today: Pay close attention to the warning sign that God places in front of you. It is always good to slow down, to step back to evaluate your life, and to listen to the Father's voice. Pay attention to what frustrates you, what drains you, and what schemes the devil likes to use to tempt you. Be aware, but don't get stuck there. Move forward in Christ and drink of Him. Spend time soaking in the presence of God and enjoying His company.

He's Been There

Hebrews 4:15: "For we do not have a high priest who is unable to empathize with our weakness, but we have one who has been tempted in every way, just as we are, yet he did not sin."

This life can be so hard at times. There are so many difficult times, struggles, and temptations that come our way. The Bible says that God is close to the brokenhearted and saves those who are crushed in spirit. Jesus specializes in fixing broken lives. I have a buddy that owns a body shop. He and his employees restore cars and trucks that have been involved with a wreck or accident. So many people bring their wrecked cars to his body shop, all mangled and smashed up. He takes his time and begins the process of restoring that vehicle. He will replace certain parts, push out dents, and buff out scratches. It may take a couple of days, but it will make it look brand new. Jesus will do the same with broken lives; He is in the restoration business.

One thing I love about Jesus is He understands what it is like to live life here on earth. He understands what it is like to be betrayed by someone you love. His heart was broken, and He also faced every temptation known to man by Satan himself. He doesn't just know about our pain; He knows our pain. He experienced enormous pain when He suffered on that cross where He bled and died. On that cross He spread out his arms to show us just how much He loved us. He loves you so much and He cares about what you are going through. He has been there and done that. But the good news is: He has overcome it all.

Challenge for today: Remind yourself that Jesus understands what you are going through. He has walked in your shoes. He has faced everything you have experienced in this life. Say out loud today, "He loves me." Say it repeatedly. He wants to restore you and make you brand new. Allow Him to buff you out and shine you up. Don't forget, it will not happen overnight. Be patient.

Lacking Nothing

I want to share a couple of verses, and a quick thought with you today. Proverbs 28:25-27: "A greedy man stirs up dissension, but he who trusts in the Lord will prosper. He who trusts in himself is a fool, but he who walks in wisdom is kept safe. He who gives to the poor will lack nothing, but he who closes his eyes to them receives many curses."

I want to ask you two questions today. First, in whom do you place your trust? Is it in yourself, in your own wisdom and strength? Or is your trust in the God of the universe? He is trustworthy, and He has all the credentials needed to be trusted. Place your life in His powerful and loving hands. Proverbs 3:5-6: "Trust in the Lord with all your heart and lean not on your own understanding; in all your ways acknowledge him, and he will make your paths straight."

Second, are you meeting the needs of people around us? Matthew 9:35-36: "Jesus went through all the towns and villages, teaching in their synagogues, preaching the good news of the kingdom and healing every disease and sickness. When he saw the crowds, he had compassion on them, because they were harassed and helpless, like a sheep without a shepherd."

Jesus not only saw the needs of the people, He met the needs of those around Him. Do we take our eyes off ourselves long enough to see the hurt, and the pain that so many carry? Not only physical needs, but spiritual needs too. Be generous to the poor and you'll never go hungry. Trust the Lord with your entire being and take time to meet the needs of people around you. Then you will lack nothing.

Challenge for today: Ask yourself this question, "Where do you place your trust or in whom do you place your trust?" Identify the things in your life that cause you worry or stress. What are you carrying that is weighing you down and has caused you great pain? Take your eyes off the situation and turn them to the Lord of the Universe. When you trust Him with everything, you have more time to see the needs of others.

Glorify Your Father

I want to share a very powerful verse with you today. Matthew 5:14-16: "You are the light of the world. A city on a hill cannot be hidden. Neither do people light a lamp and put it under a bowl. Instead they put it on its stand, and it gives light to everyone in the house. In the same way, let your light shine before others, that they may see your good deeds and glorify your Father in heaven."

In other words, we're invited to live in such a way that the world doesn't merely see that we do good things, but that we do good things because we're in a relationship with a perfect Father. We are children of the King, and our identity as sons and daughters of God unlocks prison doors, heals wounds, and propels us into greater purpose in our lives. Let your light shine in such a way that it will bring glory to your loving Heavenly Father.

There is a wealth of promises that can only be experienced when we choose to lay down our own glory and live for the glory of God instead. We were not created to live out our own advancement or promotion; that only brings future suffering and struggles. If we choose instead to seek His glory, to lift Him up and lead others to Him, we will find ultimate peace, purpose, and joy for our lives. Look what David wrote in Psalm 63:2-3, "I have seen you in the sanctuary and beheld your power and your glory. Because your love is better than life, my lips will glorify you."

Let what you say and how you live your life, speak volumes to the world and give Him the glory He deserves. Romans 15:5-6: "May the God who gives endurance and encouragement give you a spirit of unity among yourselves as you follow Christ Jesus, so that with one heart and mouth you may glorify the God and Father of our Lord Jesus Christ."

Challenge for today: Walk through life with your eyes wide open and ask God to give you an opportunity to serve others. Reflect the light, so that others will see His love. Live life in such a way that He receives all the glory.

Seasoning

Why has God placed you here on this earth? Have you ever stopped long enough to ponder this question? You're here to be salt-seasoning that brings out the God-flavors of this earth. If you lose your saltiness, how will people taste godliness? You've lost your usefulness and will end up in the garbage. Here is another way to put it. You are here to be light, bringing out the God colors in this world. God is not a secret to be kept. We're going public with this, as public as a city on a hill. If I make you light-bearers, you don't think I'm going to hide you under a bucket, do you? I'm putting you on a light stand. Shine. Keep an open house, be generous with your lives. Open your life to others and you'll prompt people to open-up with God, our generous Father in heaven. Matthew 5:13: "You are the salt of the earth. But if the salt loses its saltiness, how can it be made salty again? It is no longer good for anything, except to be thrown out and trampled by men."

I love to cook chicken on the grill. If someone is coming to our house to visit us, most likely I will break out the grill and cook chicken and vegetables. If I am in a rush and I am pressed for time, I will take the chicken and the vegetables out of the refrigerator and slap it on the grill. Yes, I will eat it and it will fill me up, no doubt, but if I really want to take it to the next level, I will go the extra mile. I would take time to marinate the chicken, and let it soak for a few hours. I would add extra seasoning to the vegetable and take my time cooking it. It will make a huge difference. It would add tons of flavor. It's all about the preparation. Take time to marinate in God's goodness and let the world experience the wonderful flavor of God.

Challenge for today: You are the light of the world; Christ lives in you. Let your light shine as you walk through life. Let others know about His amazing grace and mercy. Let them see the joy He brings to life. Don't keep this treasure to yourself but share Him with everyone you know. Live in such a way that your life will bring glory to Him. Have a great week and shine brightly.

Look at Your Tree

You don't get wormy apples off a healthy tree, nor good apples off a diseased tree. The health of the apple tree tells the health of the apple. You must begin with your own life-giving life. It's who you are, not what you say and do, that counts. Your true being brims over into your words and deeds. Jesus asked, "Why are you so polite with me, always saying yes sir, but never doing a thing I tell you?" These words I speak to you are not mere additions to your life. They are foundational words, words to build life on.

James 3:10: "Out of the same mouth come praise and cursing. My brother, this should not be."

For out of the overflow of our heart, our mouth speaks. Is our heart aligned with the Spirit of God? Does our praise on Sunday match with what we do on Friday night? Are we living a life that will make our Heavenly Father smile? Let's be real with ourselves and honest with the Lord. It's time to take self-off the throne of our life and live a life that brings Glory to the Father. Spend as much time in God's Word and prayer as you can and allow God to take over. Give Him the controls of your heart and tell Him to steer your life. What does your fruit look like this morning? Just asking.

Look at Jesus' words in Matthew 7:15-20: "Watch out for false prophets. They come to you in sheep's clothing, but inwardly they are ferocious wolves. By their fruit you will recognize them. Do people pick grapes from thorn bushes, or figs from thistles? Likewise, every good tree bears good fruit. A good tree cannot bear bad fruit, and a bad tree cannot bear good fruit. Every tree that does not bear good fruit is cut down and thrown into the fire. Thus, by their fruits you will recognize them."

Challenge for today: Ask yourself some difficult questions. Does your life match up with what you profess to believe? Are you walking out what you believe is the truth? Does your walk match your talk? Can this world see Jesus in you? Be consistent in your walk with Christ. Let people see Jesus when they look at the way you live your life.

Living A Guilt Free Life

Proverbs 28:13: "You will never succeed in life if you try to hide your sins. Confess them and give them up; then God will show mercy to you."

Guilt will chew you up and spit you out. The great accuser will put a guilt trip on you and never look back. Here is the good news: God forgives, and He shows mercy for those who are in Christ. That is what I am talking about. Here are three things we need to know about God's forgiveness.

1. God forgives instantly. First John 1:9: "If we confess our sins, he is faithful and just and will forgive us our sins and purify us from all righteousness."

You can take that to the bank. Thank you, Lord.

2. God forgives freely. Ephesians 2:8-9: "For it is by grace you have been saved, through faith, and this is not of yourselves, it is the gift of God, not of works, so that one can boast."

Romans 6:23: "For the wages of sin is death, but the gift of God is eternal life in Jesus Christ our Lord."

Think about this; both heaven and hell are full of people who are loved by God. The only difference is that the ones in heaven received what God freely gave.

3. God forgives completely. First John 2:1-2: "My dear children, I write this to you so that you will not sin. But if anybody does sin, we have an advocate with the Father-Jesus Christ, the Righteous One. He is the atoning sacrifice for our sins, and not only for ours but also for the sins of the whole world."

Check out this good news in Jeremiah 31:34, "For I will forgive their wickedness and remember their sins no more."

Never forget, God is not mad at you, but He is mad about you.

Challenge for today: Don't walk around covered with guilt but know that you have been set free because of the blood of Jesus Christ. Recognize how Satan has trapped you in guilt in the past. Don't fall for the same trap repeatedly. Say this repeatedly today, "I am free indeed."

Psalm 119:1-8

You're blessed when you stay on course, walking steadily on the road revealed by God. You're blessed when you follow His directions, doing your best to find Him. That's right, you don't go off on your own, you walk straight along the road He set. Lord, you have prescribed the right way to live; now you expect us to live it. Oh, that my steps might be steady, keeping to the course you set. Then I'd never have any regrets in comparing my life with your counsel. I thank you for speaking straight from the heart, I learn the pattern of your righteous ways. I'm going to do what you tell me to do; don't ever walk off and leave me.

Psalm 119:1-8: "Blessed are they whose ways are blameless, who walk according to the law of the Lord. Blessed are they who keep his statutes and seek him with all their heart. They do nothing wrong; they walk in his ways. You have laid down precepts that are to be fully obeyed. Oh, that my ways were steadfast in obeying your decrees! Then I would not be put to shame when I consider all your commands. I will praise you with an upright heart as I learn your righteous laws. I will obey your decrees; do not utterly forsake me."

God's Word is rich and full of wisdom. I hate to admit it, but I am not good with following instructions. I hate when I buy something, and I must put it together. Yes, it has instructions, but I feel I can look at it, and figure it out faster than taking the time to read the instructions. For some reason, I always have spare pieces left and I always skip over a step or two. It all looks so easy, but somehow, I always seem to mess it up. Too many times, I want to take the short cuts that end up costing me more time. Maybe I should start reading the instructions, it may save me a lot of headaches? How many times have we done life our way and we haven't taken the time to read the instruction book?

Challenge for today: I encourage you to take time to read His instructions and try doing things His way. It will save you a lot of headaches.

His Trademark

Psalm 145:17-21: "The Lord is righteous in all his ways and loving toward all he has made. The Lord is near to all who call on him, to all who call on him in truth. He fulfills the desires of those who fear him: he hears their cry and saves them. The Lord watches over all who love him, but all the wicked he will destroy. My mouth will speak in praise of the Lord. Let every creature praise his holy name for ever and ever."

Everything God does is right; the trademark on all his work is love. First John 4:16-19: "God is love. Whoever lives in love lives in God, and God in him. In this way, love is made complete among us so that we will have confidence on the day of judgment, because in this world we are like him. There is no fear in love. But perfect love drives out fear, because fear has to do with punishment. The one who fears is not made in perfect love. We love because he first loved us."

God is there, listening for all who pray. Call out to Him. He does what is best for those who fear Him. He hears our cry, and He feels our hurt. He understands what we are facing. God sticks by all who love Him, but it is all over for those who don't. My mouth is full of God's praise. Let everything living bless Him, bless His holy name from now to eternity.

Challenge for today: Call out to the God of love and compassion. Tell Him what is going on in your life, and the different struggles that you are facing. He cares, and He is faithful. It is time to unload all the baggage of life and surrender it all to the Lord. Stop carrying that heavy load and lay it at His feet. Then praise Him. He desires it.

Psalm 119:9-12

Psalm 119:9-12: "How can a young man keep his way pure? By living according to your word. I seek you with all my heart; do not let me stray from your commands. I have hidden your word in my heart that I may not sin against you. Praise be to you, O Lord; teach me your decrees."

How can a young man live a clean life? Look at what Paul writes in First Peter 1:13-16: "Therefore, prepare your minds for action; be self-controlled; set your hope fully on the grace to be given you when Jesus Christ is revealed. As obedient children, do not conform to the evil desires you had when you lived in ignorance. But just as he who called you is holy, so be holy in all you do; for it is written: 'Be holy, because I am holy.'"

That almost seems impossible these days. We live in a world where there is temptation on every corner, and evil lurks in the shadows waiting to pounce on you. It can be done, but we must pay close attention to the road map of God's Word. He must be our single pursuit. Don't miss the road signs the Lord will put in front of you during the journey. Lock these directions in your heart and secure them in your vault. Never let them go. His road map will keep us headed in the right direction to arrive at our final destination safely. Hebrews 4:12: "For the word of God is living and active. Sharper than any double-edged sword, it penetrates even to dividing soul and spirit, joint and marrow; it judges the thoughts and attitudes of the heart."

Challenge for today: Pick up God's Word, this is God's love letter to us. In His Word we can find directions to a life of fulfillment, peace, and great joy, even when we are in the middle of chaos. How can we keep our ways pure? By living according to His Word. This is the truth, and we can bank on it.

The Verse

Deuteronomy 6:4-5: "The Lord our God, the Lord is one. Love the Lord God with all your heart and with all your soul and with all your strength."

We need to put this in front of our faces every day. We need to run through this verse over, and over again throughout the day. It is one thing to read this verse, but it is another thing to apply it, and to live it out. Has this verse ever come alive in your heart? This is a call to put God on the throne of your heart, and to make Him Lord of your life. This is so much more than going to church every Sunday and Wednesday. It's about giving God first place in all that you do. It's about practicing His presence and serving Him 24 hours a day. It is giving Him all that He deserves and giving Him glory for what He has done in our lives. It is about going all in and holding nothing back.

Matthew 6:33: "But seek first his kingdom and his righteousness, and all these things will be given to you as well."

Ecclesiastes 12:13: Fear God and keep his commandments, for this is the whole duty of man."

Romans 12:1-2: Therefore, I urge you, brothers, in the view of God's mercy, to offer your bodies as living sacrifices, holy and pleasing to God-this is your spiritual act of worship. Do not conform any longer to the pattern of this world but be transformed by the renewing of your mind. Then you will be able to test and approve what God's will is-his good, pleasing and perfect will."

Challenge for today: Memorize Deuteronomy 6:4-5. I encourage you to let this verse sink in. Don't just read it and move on. Write it out on a piece of paper and put it on your desk at work or on the dash of your car. Take time to pray over this verse. Ask the Lord, "What does this look like in my life? What needs to change for this verse to come alive in me?"

What's the Root?

What is the difference between forgiveness and cleansing? Have you ever stopped to think about that? The best way to illustrate the difference between the two has to do with cutting grass. It's the difference between cutting the weed off at the root and just mowing over it. You see, forgiveness has to do with the result of sin. Cleaning has to do with the cause of sin. Forgiveness comes by confession and restitution. Cleaning comes by walking in the light and being in the presence of God.

First John 1:5-9: "This is the message we have heard from him and declared to you: God is light; in him there is no darkness at all. If we claim to have fellowship with him yet walk in darkness, we lie and do not live by truth. But if we walk in the light, as he is in the light, we have fellowship with one another, and the blood of Jesus, his Son, purifies us from all sin. If we claim to be without sin, we deceive ourselves and the truth is not in us. If we confess our sins, he is faithful and just and will forgive us our sins and purify us from all unrighteousness."

First Timothy 6:9-12: "People who want to get rich fall into temptation and a trap and into many foolish and harmful desires that plunge men into ruin and destruction. For the love of money is a root of all kinds of evil. Some people, eager for money, have wandered from the faith and pierced themselves with many griefs. But you, man of God, flee from all this, and pursue righteousness, godliness, faith, love, endurance, and gentleness. Fight the good fight of faith."

To walk in the Light means God will ask us to make lifestyle changes including the way we use our time, how we talk, and who we put first in our lives. Run from sin and pursue the very One who loves you the most. His name is Jesus.

Challenge for today: Ask God to show you the root of your sin. Then walk in close fellowship with the Father. You will not regret it. I hope you have a great day.

Pure Heart

I hope you are doing well. John 3:30: "He must become greater; I must become less."

This short verse really packs a punch. Think about this, God must increase, and I must decrease. Oh, how we need to die to self and crave a pure heart.

Let's start it off with a question. What do you think of when you hear the word pure? Most think of purity as the elimination of evil or the absence of contamination. That is true, but the second part that is often left off is the desire and commitment to one thing. For instance, take pure gold. Not only is pure gold free of dirt and grime, but it is also free from other valuable things such as silver or diamonds. A pure heart is a heart that wills, seeks, and wants one thing. It's where every decision and every choice are totally surrendered to God. God yearns for us to have a pure heart.

Jeremiah 29:13: "You will seek me and find me when you seek me with all your heart."

We need our time alone with God daily. A time of confession and repentance. Turn your back on sin and walk away from the schemes of the devil. "Thank you, Jesus, for making a way in the darkness and providing a way of salvation." David prayed in Psalm 51:7-12: "Cleanse me with hyssop, and I will be clean; wash me, and I will be whiter than snow. Let me hear joy and gladness; let the bones you have crushed rejoice. Hide your face from my sins and blot out all my iniquity. Create in me a pure heart, O God, and renew a steadfast spirit within me. Do not cast me from your presence or take your Holy Spirit from me. Restore to me the joy of your salvation and grant me a willing spirit to sustain me."

Challenge for today: Are you all in? What does your heart look like? I pray over you a pure heart that wills, seeks, and wants one thing, a heart that is surrounded by God.

Discover Your Gift

In 1934, a revival took place in North Carolina. Two teenage boys walked up to the tent, heard the music and decided to walk in. Mordecai Ham spoke that night. He didn't have a book deal and he never appeared on TV. Both boys that night received Christ. One of those boys was Billy Graham. Mordecai Ham was doing what he was called to do, and God blessed his efforts. Nothing is more draining than trying to do what God has not wired you to do. Discover your gifts, lower stress, and increase your joy. I want to share with you four steps to find and use your gifts. Don't forget, God hasn't gifted anybody to do everything.

1. Decide: You will never possess what you are not willing to pursue. Make up your mind to serve God. Make a commitment to use your gift for His glory.
2. Discover: Spend time in prayer, asking God to help you tap into what He has given you. Talk to other godly people and ask their opinion of your gift. Discover all the different spiritual gifts that God provides His children with. Find out what brings you great joy.
3. Develop: When you discover your gifting from God, work hard to develop it. Practice, practice, practice. Take time to learn from others who have done it for a long time.
4. Deploy: Let God lead you and take control. Take your gift and put it into service.

What if Mordecai Ham never decided to use his gift? What if he decided to do his own thing because preaching looked too hard, and he really didn't like speaking in front of a lot of people.

Challenge for today: Decide, Discover, Develop, and Deploy your gift and get moving for the glory of the Lord.

What Really Matters to You?

Whost place does Jesus occupy in your heart? Does He have the top priority, or do we give Him the leftovers? Our dog, Miles, loves to sit at my wife's feet while we eat dinner. She sits there because she knows if she is patient and waits, she will get some scraps from her plate. Jesus deserves more than scraps from our plates; He deserves a royal feast. He deserves our very best. The fact is, we give our best to less deserving things. How many times do we skip our time alone with God to check our Facebook or our Instagram account? Matthew 6:33: "But seek first his kingdom and his righteousness, and all these things will be given to you as well."

Who is sitting on the throne of your heart? Is it self or is it Christ?

This world has it all backwards. It tries to tell us to do "all these things" and fit God in where you can. The world tells us we don't need to go to church and worship; you can just watch it on a video because it is just as good. Yes, you may hear a good message, but where is the accountability and the commitment? Are you encouraging the body of Christ sitting in your PJs at the house? Are you using your gift to encourage other believers that day? If we make a commitment to live for God alone, and we daily revisit and live by that decision, we will do more of what matters most and less of what doesn't. Let's get our focus back to what matters most - Jesus.

Challenge for today: Ask yourself these questions: What consumes your thoughts? What really matters to you? What are you pursuing and chasing? Take time to examine your heart and to honestly look at your life and your priorities. Does Jesus take first place in your life?

Three Things: Check It Out

Romans 10:17: "Consequently, faith comes from hearing the message, and the message is heard through the Word of Christ." Did you catch that? Faith comes from hearing and knowing God's Word. So, consider these three things when it comes to God's Word.

1. God's Word is our food.

If we want to experience the real, abundant, eternal life that Jesus offers, the only way is to consume his Word every day. The same way your body needs food, our soul needs Jesus. A steady diet of scripture is to the soul what a steak and potato is to the body. Fill your soul with the Word of God.

2. God's Word is our weapon.

Hebrews 4:12: "For the Word of God is alive and active. Sharper than any double-edged sword, it penetrates even to divide soul and spirit, joints and marrow; it judges the thoughts and attitudes of the heart."

When we face a spiritual attack or temptation, we can fight back using the Word of God as our weapon. We cannot always prevent the attack, but we can prepare for it and be ready to use God's Word in our defense. His Word is a powerful weapon.

3. The Word of God is our guide.

Psalm 119:105: "Your word is a lamp for my feet, a light on my path."

In a dark world, when nothing is certain, when all you see are shadows, and you're not sure which way to go, the Word of God is the light you need to make it to your destination. Maybe you have gotten off course. Maybe your life has been hijacked by the enemy and your dreams have been crushed. You have ended up in a place you never thought you would be. God's Word will lead you back to the center of His love.

Challenge for today: Consume it, fight your battles with it, and follow it as your guide. Great faith comes when we decide that His Word is enough. Devour the Word of God. It's our daily spiritual food we need to be strong to continue to fight in this spiritual war with Satan. Dig in.

Contend For Your Faith

Take a deep breath and thank God for three things today. Take time to give Him a little praise and love on Him today.

In Jude 1:3-4: "Dear friends, although I was very eager to write to you about the salvation we share, I felt I had to write and urge you to contend for the faith that was once for all entrusted to the saints. For certain whose condemnation was written about long ago have secretly slipped in. They are godless men, who changed the grace of our God into a license for immortality and deny Jesus Christ our only Sovereign and Lord."

False teachers slipped into the early church and shared a false doctrine. Jude was begging the early Church to fight and contend for their faith in Jesus Christ. Fight with everything you have and stand for truth.

He went on to write Jude 1:20-23: "Dear friends, build yourselves up in your most holy faith and pray in the Holy Spirit. Keep yourselves in God's love as you wait for the mercy of our Lord Jesus Christ to bring you eternal life. Be merciful to those who doubt; snatch others from the fire and save them, to others show mercy, mixed with fear-hating even the clothing stained by corrupted flesh."

Stay right in the center of God's love and stand your ground. Keep fighting.

Challenge for today: Keep your arms open and outstretched to those who need to know about the amazing love of Jesus Christ. Hang in there, Church. Don't grow weary and give up. Keep on fighting and keep on sharing. It's worth the fight.

Let This Sink In

The God of the impossible, the Creator of heaven and earth, the Alpha and the Omega, knows me by name. Not only does He know my name, but He knows everything about me. Psalm 139:1-4: "O Lord, you have searched me and you know me. You know when I sit and when I rise; you perceive my heart thoughts from afar. You discern my going out and my lying down; you are familiar with all my ways. Before a word is on my tongue you know it completely, O Lord."

Even when we are unaware of His presence. He is still watching, working, and guiding us to Himself. That's my God.

Check out Psalm 122:1-3: "I lift up my eyes to the hills-where does my help come from? My help comes from the Lord, the Maker of heaven and earth. He will not let your foot slip-He who watches over you will not slumber."

He created the Blue Ridge Mountains, the Grand Canyon, and He hung the sun in just the right place, but we are His masterpiece. To be loved by God is our greatest privilege. Let that sink in. May God bless you and know that you are loved by the very Creator of heaven and earth.

Challenge for today: Know that you are God's greatest treasure. Say these words to your Heavenly Father, "Thanks for loving me." Say it repeatedly. Thank Him for two blessings and give some honor and praise for who He is, and what He has done for us. He knows you better than you know yourself.

Soaring Or Sinking?

Why are some people more effective than others? Why do some soar while others sink? Why do some thrive emotionally, seem happier, and more fulfilled? I know, those are some hard questions to answer, but it is worth the effort to think this through. Romans 15:13: "May the God of hope fill you with all joy and peace as you trust in Him, so that you may overflow with hope by the power of the Holy Spirit."

Thriving people thrive for one reason: They commit to things that produce inner strength and hope. One last question, what is the source of your hope? True and lasting hope is found only in a person. His name is Jesus. What are you committed to? Is it producing strength and hope in your life? It's time to walk in a different path, and it's time to plug in to a new power source. It is time to push selfishness and pride aside and surrender to the One who owns it all. It is time to thrive. I pray that your joy may be full today to a point of overflowing.

Challenge for today: Commit Romans 15:13 to memory. Say this verse repeatedly in your mind. Then ask God what this means for your life, and how you can walk this out. We need hope by the power of the Holy Spirit not just to get by, but to thrive. It is time to soar, it is time to dream, and it is a time to push forward to reach a lost and dying world for the glory of God. I pray that your soul will be full to overflowing with hope in Jesus' name.

Is It Getting Worse?

I grew up in East Albany, Georgia and I attended Dougherty High School. There I played baseball, football and enjoyed being called a River Rat. My tenth-grade year, I attended my first summer camp for football. The head football coach's name was Luther Welsh. He wasn't a big man in stature, but he was very intimidating to say the least. He didn't mind getting in your face and letting you know what he thought. That summer camp lasted two weeks, and we had to spend the night in the school gym. We had three practices a day. If that wasn't enough, we also had a weight workout too.

Those two weeks seemed like it would never end. I can remember all the bumps, bruises, cuts, and the scrapes. I had a buddy who scraped up his knee badly that first week. I kept telling him to go and see the coach about it, because it was starting to look gross. He kept saying, "It's nothing, it's just a little scrape." Well, he continued to ignore the pain, and kept going to every practice three times a day. By the end of the week, he could barely walk. One of the coaches noticed there was something going on and asked, "What is wrong with you?" My friend pointed to his knee, and the coach pulled his knee pad up to see the grossest sore you would ever want to see. Because he ignored the pain, and didn't get any help, that small scrape turned into staph infection. There are no words to describe what my buddy had to go through that next hour, and I watched it all. A wound that is neglected gets infected.

When you experience pain, you must deal with whatever is causing it. Ignoring it will not make it go away. It will only get worse. When you are facing a hard time and experiencing pain, don't carry it alone. Talk to someone and unload. Let the people who love you help. It's ok to ask for help. What do you need to share with a friend?

First Peter 5:6-7: "Humble yourselves, therefore, under God's mighty hand, that he may lift you up in due time. Cast all your anxiety on him, because he cares for you."

Challenge for today: Are you convinced that Jesus cares for you? Until you are convinced, you will never cast your cares on Him. Drop the pride and humble yourself before your Lord and expose your wounds and your hurt. Stop trying to hide it, and hand it to the Lord. Let God's love flow over you and allow that wound to be cleansed and to be healed. A wound that is neglected gets infected.

The Americanized Gospel

I want to unload something and get it off my chest by asking a few questions. Are we guilty of perverting the Gospel of Jesus Christ? Has the Church today watered down His truth to the world? We seem to choose what I call the buffet style Christianity. That is where we pick and choose what we want and what suits us best. Anything less than complete surrender of our lives to the Lordship of Jesus Christ is robbing God of the glory. We want God on our terms, and that is how we get false religion. We can only encounter a vibrant relationship with God on His terms. We've got just enough of Jesus to be informed, but not enough to be transformed. Think about it: We want everything God has to offer without giving up anything.

I encourage you to read Matthew 19:16-24. This is the story of the rich, young ruler. He had everything: power, position, and money, but he was missing something. He had everything this world had to offer, but he was empty. He knew there had to be more to this life than what he was experiencing. In Matthew 19:21 Jesus told this young man, "If you want to give it all you've got, go sell everything you have and give it to the poor. Then follow me."

That was the last thing the young ruler expected to hear. He walked away holding on tight to his stuff, that he couldn't bear to let go. Be honest. Have you ever felt bad for the rich young ruler? Maybe Jesus was too hard on him? We tend to focus on what Jesus asked him to give up but we fail to consider what Jesus offered up in exchange. The young man gave up a three-year internship with Jesus, box seats to every groundbreaking sermon, and a chance to become an eyewitness to miracle after miracle.

Challenge for today: Draw a line and live a life that matters. Happiness is not found in accumulating possessions, but in pursuing an intimate relationship with Jesus Christ. The things of this world are nice, but they will leave you empty and wanting more. Only Jesus can satisfy.

That Guy

I am a very patient guy except when it comes to heavy traffic, and what some people do during those times. I am talking about "That Guy". You know, "That Guy" when traffic is bumper to bumper, and all the cars are barely moving because they have closed the far-left lane to do repairs. The closed lanes are clearly marked, but "That Guy" sees his chance to skip about 50 cars and decides to speed up and get in that closed left lane. Then he proceeds to zoom past you and other cars in front of him. But now "That Guy" must get back over when that lane runs out. Then "That Guy" tries his best to stick the nose of his car between you and the car in front of you to get back over. I try my best to squeeze him out, in Jesus' name. I know that is not very Christ-like, but that really gets under my skin. Why? Because it is not fair. If I let him get away with it, he will get something he doesn't deserve. What he deserves is to sit there and wait his turn. It's only fair, right? Is anybody with me?

But it makes me think, what if God gave us what we deserved? What if God didn't show us mercy and grace? No matter how hard we try to be good, we can't be good enough. We could never live up to God's standard. John 1:17: "For the law was given through Moses; grace and truth came through Jesus Christ."

John 3:17: "For God didn't send his Son into the world to condemn the world, but to save the world through him."

How amazing is that? Do we deserve heaven and God's grace? No, but God allowed me in line because He loved me. I didn't deserve it, but He showed me grace. God knows I could have never reached His standards, so He sent Jesus. Wow. I was "That Guy".

Challenge for today: Thank the Lord for His grace, mercy, and the gift of life found only in Jesus. Praise and worship Him.

Let's Talk About The "P" Word

Let's look at pride today. There is an old saying that goes something like this; If we are not thirsty for Christ, then we are full of ourselves, and people can tell what we are full of. Proverbs 16:18-19: "Pride goes before destruction; a haughty spirit goes before a fall. Better to be lowly in spirit and among the oppressed than to share plunder with the proud."

When we are proud, we are all about ourselves. We might think well of ourselves or poorly of ourselves, but we don't stop thinking about ourselves. Our "self" is the problem, not the solution. Jesus is the solution. If we focus on ourselves, we will have a hard time seeing Him. Proverbs 6:16-19: "There are six things the Lord hates, seven things that are detestable to him: haughty eyes, lying tongue, hands that shed innocent blood, a heart that devises wicked schemes, feet that are quick to rush to evil, false witness who pours out lies and a man who stirs up dissension among brothers."

Pride tops this list. Pride is a cancer that will destroy you from the inside out and it will spread without you even knowing it. What are we full of today? Has pride slipped in and taken over? Has God taken a back seat in your life?

Challenge for today: I encourage you to get before the Lord and get things right with Him. Confess your sin of pride and pray for forgiveness. Ask Him to show you His ways and teach you His path, and to guide you in all truth. Pride will leave you empty and alone. What are you waiting on?

Something To Celebrate

I don't know about you, but I love to celebrate. That is why I look forward to all the holidays and all the festivities that follow. If you love to celebrate too, here is a verse that needs to be celebrated. Romans 6:11-14: "In the same way, count yourselves dead to sin but alive to God in Christ Jesus. Therefore do not let your sin reign in your mortal body so that you obey its evil desires. Do not offer the parts of your body to sin, as instruments of wickedness, but rather offer yourselves to God, as those who have been brought from death to life; and offer the parts of your body to him as instruments of righteousness. For sin shall not be your master, because you are not under the law, but under grace."

If you are in Christ, you are dead to sin and alive in Him, and we need to celebrate it. This means we must not give sin a vote in the way we conduct our lives. Don't give it the time of day. Throw yourselves wholeheartedly into God's way of doing things. Sin should no longer tell you how to live your life. In Christ, we are no longer under the tyranny of the law, but we are living in the freedom of God. Let's celebrate God's amazing grace. We were bought at a price. Therefore, honor God with your body. Take care of the temple that God has blessed you with.

First Corinthians 3:16-17: "Don't you know that you yourselves are God's temple and that God's Spirit lives in you? If anyone destroys God's temple, God will destroy him; for God's temple is sacred, and you are that temple."

Challenge for today: Celebrate God's goodness. Take time now to thank God audibly for all His goodness that He has shown you over the years. Yes, say it out loud, in other words, count your many blessings, and name them one by one. He has given you a reason to celebrate; don't take His grace for granted. Where would you be without His amazing grace?

Be Bold

I have discovered over the years if you run after the Lord with all your heart, He will push you out of your comfort zone. God sometimes likes to do things the hard way. Look at the life of Moses. Moses didn't like to talk in front of people. Moses told the Lord that he was not eloquent and very slow of speech. But God called Moses to go before the most powerful man alive at that time and tell him to let His people go. Can you see Moses stumbling over his words? Moses begged God to find someone else to go before Pharaoh. Why? Because it was hard. That was not in his comfort zone.

What about Gideon? God called him to push out his enemies from the land, so Gideon gathered an army of 32,000 men to get the job done. Gideon knew he could do what God asked him to do because he was a warrior, and this is what he was gifted to do. In Judges 7, God told Gideon, "You have too many men." God narrowed it down to 300 men to accomplish this task. Now Gideon was pushed out of his comfort zone. God likes to do things the hard way. What about Jesus? Jesus came from Heaven and was born in a stable. He died on a cross and was buried in a borrowed tomb. He could have come as a Conquering King, but God likes to do things the hard way.

As a kid I loved to play ball. I really loved to play with a bouncy ball and come up with some crazy games. The bouncy ball worked best on hard surfaces. You could drop it on the hard floor, and it would bounce right back to you. It didn't work so well on carpet or a soft surface. The floor had to be hard. When hard times come, God is not punishing you. He is preparing you. God put Moses, Gideon, and Jesus in tough situations, but they all bounced back. Moses led his people out of Egypt and crossed the Red Sea. He turned around and saw his enemies floating in the Sea. Gideon bounced back and was victorious in what God called him to do. Jesus overcame sin and death and is now sitting at the right hand of God. Amen.

Challenge for today: What is God putting in front of you? Pray for opportunities to love on people and ask God for favor. Things may get hard, but never forget: God is right by your side. I pray over your boldness to face the challenges of life.

Steady My Steps

Life is full of uncertainty, strife, heart break, disappointment, and negativity. Turn on the news and see it for yourself. More than ever before, this world is overcome by depression, sadness, and hate. So how in the world can we stay positive and encouraged? How can we be a positive influence when it seems like the world is falling apart? Stay grounded in God's Word. Get the Bible off the coffee table, jump in, and dig. Put down your phone and pick up God's Book of life. God's Word is alive, active, and it will change your life forever and ever. If you need encouragement or a positive word, break open God's life manual. You will find direction and a path that leads to joy.

Psalm 119:133-136: "Direct my footsteps according to your word; let no sin rule over me. Redeem me from the oppression of men, that I may obey your precepts. May your face shine upon your servant and teach me your decrees. Streams of tears flow from thy eyes, for your law is not obeyed."

"Lord, steady our steps with your Word of promise. Rescue us from the traps of Satan so we can live life your way. Smile on us, your servants, teach us the right way to live through your Word." Amen.

Challenge for today: Make a commitment to the Lord to start your day off with a positive Word from God. This may be the area of your walk with Christ that you tend to struggle with. Ask the Lord to give you a new passion for His Word and that you will come to a point where you can't get enough. As believers in Christ, we need the fuel of God's Word to keep us going. Don't wait till your warning lights start flashing.

Don't Even Try It

Look at Romans 8:35 with me. Paul writes and says, "Who shall separate us from the love of Christ? Shall trouble or hardship or persecution or famine or nakedness or danger or sword?"

Do you think anyone is going to be able to drive a wedge between us and Christ's love? There is no way. Not trouble, nor hard time, not hatred, not even Satan's schemes. None of this fazes us because Jesus loves us. Nothing living or dead, angelic, or demonic, today, or tomorrow- absolutely nothing can get between us and God's love because of the way that Jesus has embraced us. God loved us enough to send His very best in the form of a baby. He lived the perfect life, and He willingly laid down his life on the cross. He overcame sin and death, and He bridged that gap between a Holy God and sinful man. Jesus painted a beautiful picture of who God really is. The baby in the manger took my place on that rugged cross, and He showed us all what true love is.

The devil will do everything he can to drive a wedge between you and the Lord. It drives him crazy to know that you are walking so close to the Lord. He hates to see you happy, thriving, and full of hope. He knows that only encourages others to do the same. When those troubled times come - and they will come - hold to the promises of God. Don't fall away from God, and doubt His goodness, but hold on to truth. God's Word needs to be your anchor that holds you in the hard times of life. His Word will keep you from drifting and will hold you steady in the storm. Hold on to the promise of God; there is nothing that will separate you from His love.

Challenge for today: Trust in truth that comes straight from God's Word. Never doubt His love for you. Take time now to praise Jesus' holy name and give Him some thanks for all He has done for you. Identify the lies that Satan has used on you in the past; he will most likely use some of the same tactics that have brought you down before. Ask God for wisdom and strength to overcome and for the awareness to see what may be coming your way.

The Baby That Changed Everything

It may not be Christmas when you read this, but that is ok. This verse in Isaiah is good to read all year long. This scripture is still packed with power, and it will make you stop and take notice. Isaiah 9:6: "For to us a child is born, to us a son is given, and the government will be on his shoulders. And he will be called Wonderful Counselor, Mighty God, Everlasting Father, Prince of Peace."

Everything we need is found in God's gift to us. His name is Jesus. We need to share this and stand on it twelve months out of the year. John 1:1-5: "In the beginning was the Word, and the Word was with God, and the Word was God. He was with God in the beginning. Through him all things were made; without him nothing was made that has been made. In him was life, and that life was the light of men. The light shines in the darkness, but the darkness has not understood it."

Jesus is the True Vine, the Prince of Peace, the Faithful One, the Bread of Life, and my personal Savior. In Him, there is life. In Him there is forgiveness and grace. He was the Gift that God sent to all mankind. My question is, have you received him? A gift is only a gift if you will receive it. This baby changed everything. Matthew 1:21: "She will give birth to a son, and you are to give him the name Jesus, because he will save his people from their sins."

Challenge for today: Say this out loud, "He is all I need, Jesus is enough." Say those words three more times. Thank God for His goodness, His faithfulness, and the hope we have received because of what Jesus has done for us. Baby Jesus changed everything, and I have experienced His grace.

What Makes You an Overcomer?

Let's look at First John 5:1-5, "Everyone who believes that Jesus is the Christ is born of God, and everyone who loves the Father loves his child as well. This is how we know that we love the children of God: by loving God and carrying out his commands. This is love for God: to obey his commands. And His commands are not burdensome, for everyone born of God overcomes the world. This is the victory that has overcome the world, even our faith. Who is it that overcomes the world? Only he who believes that Jesus is the Son of God."

This is a very needed word in our lives today. Man working for God is one thing, but God working in man is quite another. What we have in our world today is a system of religion that encourages us to work for God. This kind of work is frustrating and fruitless most of the time. But when we finally see the truth, it is God who works in man. This truth will be the game changer. Victory is a gift I receive in the person of Jesus Christ. Victory is not something I win, but Someone I receive in my life. John asked a very important question, "Who is it that overcomes the world?" How will you answer this question? Only the one who believes that Jesus is the Son of God can experience true victory. That is not my opinion, but that is straight from the Word of God.

Challenge for today: Make a list of those things that you struggle with. What mountains are sitting right in front of you? Are you trusting God for the strength and the wisdom to overcome? I encourage you not to shrink back and withdraw from the challenge. There is victory in a relationship with Jesus Christ. He has given you everything you need to overcome.

The Gift of Forgiveness

It would be great if we could get along with everybody, but we all will have a few run-ins along the way. There will be times when we will need to forgive, and forgiveness will be the last thing on our minds. I want to share Colossians 3:12-14 with you. It says, "As God's chosen people, holy and dearly loved, clothe yourself with compassion and kindness, humility, gentleness, and patience. Bear with each other and forgive whatever grievance you may have against one another. Forgive as the Lord forgave you."

Another version says, "Chosen by God for this new life of love, dress in the wardrobe God picked out for you: compassion, kindness, humility, quiet strength, discipline. Be ever tempered, content with second place, quick to forgive an offense. Forgive as quickly and completely as the Master forgave you."

It may be hard to receive this word, but God has put this in front of you for a reason. Who do you need to forgive? Matthew 5:23-24: "If you are offering your gift at the altar and there remember that your brother has something against you, leave your gift there in front of the altar. First go and be reconciled to your brother; then come and offer your gift."

That is not an opinion, but those are the words of Jesus himself. Whose face has God placed before you? I encourage you to swallow your pride, put on love, and be obedient to what God is telling you to do. Never forget what God has forgiven you.

Challenge of today: Write down the names of those who God has placed on your heart. Sit back and take a deep breath. Then ask God what you need to do to make these relationships right. Don't put it off.

Plug It In

When we accept Jesus as our Lord and Savior, we are in a secure relationship with God that cannot be altered. John 10:27-28: "My sheep listen to my voice; I know them, and they follow me. I give them eternal life, and they will never perish; no one can snatch them out of my hand."

That is a promise from the lips of Jesus. Because of Jesus, we have fellowship with God, and we become part of His family. As God's children, we have the privilege to call on Him for wisdom and strength. But keep in mind, our union with God depends on His grace. There is nothing we can do to earn this favor. We are now connected to the greatest power source known to man because of our relationship to Jesus Christ.

I vacuum my house about three times a week. I don't enjoy it, but it is just something I do. What would happen if I took that vacuum cleaner and pushed it all over my house, and I covered every square inch of my floor. But I forgot to plug it in. What good would I have done? I would just be going through the motions and would have wasted a lot of energy and accomplished nothing. I must plug my vacuum cleaner into the power source to be effective. As the Church, we need to get plugged into the ultimate power source. We are trying to do the work of God through our own strength and power. Most of the time, we are just going through the motions and wasting so much energy and not believing God for the impossible. Jesus spoke these words in John 14:12-14, "I tell you the truth, anyone who has faith in me will do what I have been doing. He will do even greater things than these, because I am going to the Father. And I will do whatever you ask in my name, so that the Son may bring glory to the Father."

Does that blow you away? It should. It's time to get plugged in, Church. Dive deep into God's Word and stand on His promises. Pray big prayers that could only be accomplished through the power of God.

Challenge for today: Dream big because we have a BIG God. Don't back down or shrink back but get plugged in and allow the power of the Holy Spirit to empower you. "Thank you, Lord, for your grace and the privilege to be a child of God."

The Real Power Source

There are many options to energize all the things in your life. Your home is powered by a certain power company, and your watch is powered by a small, little battery. We are constantly charging the battery of our cell phones. Sometimes those power sources let us down. Have you ever been enjoying a show on TV and resting in your nice, cool home on a hot summer day and the power goes off? We all have been there. We begin to ask, "What is going on?" Most of the time it was the best part of the movie or right before our favorite team was about to score. What do we do now?

Acts 2:1-2: "When the day of Pentecost came, they were all together in one place. Suddenly a sound like the blowing of a violent wind came from heaven and filled the whole house where they were sitting."

Our power is the Holy Spirit. It is a power source that will never go out. Do we take the Holy Spirit for granted, or do we tap into Him daily? The indwelling of the Holy Spirit was given to us to provide access to the power source that can meet all our needs. If you are in Christ, God has promised you His Presence through the power of the Holy Spirit. Lord, kill me. Not literally of course but help me to die of selfishness and pride. Then fill me with your Holy Spirit. Help me to be a container that is pleasing in Your eyes. The good news is this: His power source is unlimited, and we don't have to pay a monthly bill.

Challenge for today: I want you to pray a simple prayer that says this, "Lord, kill me, then fill me." Simply ask God to show you what rules your heart, and then hand it over to Him. He has called His children to die to selfishness and pride. Don't stop there. Now ask Him to fill you up with the power of the Holy Spirit to a point of overflowing. Walk in power.

Your Rights?

Philippians 2:7-8: "Jesus made himself nothing, taking the very nature of a servant, being in human likeness. And being found in appearance as a man, he humbled himself and became obedient to death-even death on a cross."

There is no greater example of humility than Jesus. He laid down His royal position to pursue you and me. Think about this, He knew He would be betrayed, spit on, and hung on a cross. He came anyway. Jesus gave up His rights, to obey God and to serve us. Jesus made the ultimate sacrifice and willingly laid down His life on an old rugged cross. Jesus, the Son of God, the picture of ultimate power, humbly set His rights aside. He chose humility because he loves perfectly. Love was his motivation.

What "rights" are you hanging on to today? Know this, when we lay down our rights, we pick up His righteousness. Our broken world is desperately seeking the hope we have in Jesus. Love came down from Heaven in its purest form. Jesus, your love overwhelms me today. Let us never lose the wonder of your great love. David knew of the great love that God had for him when he wrote Psalm 40:1-4: "I waited patiently for the Lord; he turned to me and heard my cry. He lifted me out of the slimy pit, out of the mud and mire; he set my feet on the rock and gave me a firm place to stand. He put a new song in my mouth, a hymn of praise to our God. Many will see and fear and put their trust in the Lord. Blessed is the man who makes the Lord his trust, who does not look to the proud, to those who turn aside to false gods."

Challenge for today: Thank God for His unmeasurable love and grace. Take time to remember what His grace has covered in your life. What pit has He pulled you out of? Thank Him for the gift of Jesus and what that has meant in you. Ask God to expose selfishness and pride that lives in your heart and then have a time of confession.

What Are You Giving for Christmas?

When I am talking with kids around Christmas, I find myself asking this question, "What are you getting for Christmas?" I love seeing their eyes light up, and the smile that comes across their faces. I don't know about you, but I have so many great childhood memories of Christmas Day. I couldn't wait to see what Santa Claus was going to bring me. I want to ask you a different question, "What are you giving for Christmas this year?"

If I were to be honest, the Christian life is inconvenient, full of detours, and rarely simple. In other words, genuine service is rooted in what we do for others, not what others can do for us. What have we done lately that serves others when we didn't get anything in return? As followers of Christ, we have an opportunity to radically change the world. Let this Christmas, even though it may be months away, let it be more about what we give, than what we get. Jesus came to seek and to save those who were lost, and to help us to do the same. Lord, give us the eyes to see those who need you. Give us your heart to serve others and use us as your hands and feet.

First John 3:16: "This is how we know what love is: Jesus Christ laid down his life for us. And we ought to lay down our life for our brothers."

What are you giving for Christmas?

Challenge for today: Christmas should affect us more than one month out of the year. It should touch our hearts all year long. Take time to look at those around you. Put on the eyes of Christ and see the needs of those who need a touch of Jesus. Look for opportunities to give Jesus away.

Delight in the Word

I want to share a word with you that is from Psalm 119:9-16: "How can a young man keep his way pure? By living according to your word. I seek you with all my heart; do not let me stray from your commands. I have hidden your word in my heart that I might not sin against you. Praise be to you, O Lord; teach me your decrees. With my lips I recount all the laws that come from your mouth. I rejoice in following your statutes as one rejoices in great riches. I meditate on your precepts and consider your ways. I delight in your decrees; I will not neglect your word."

There is nothing better than a hot brownie coming out of the oven. It fills the house with an incredible aroma, and I can't wait to place it in my mouth. I can guarantee you I will not eat it fast, but I will savor it and enjoy it. I will delight myself with that brownie.

The writer of Psalm 119 asks a simple question, "How can a young man keep his way pure?" This world is full of evil and deception. and Satan is on the attack. He knows his time is short, and he is out to destroy you and your family. I have seen so many Christians walk away from God and His Church. It breaks my heart; I can only imagine what it does to the Lord. How can we stay strong? How can we overcome temptation and the schemes of the devil? How can we stay on track and focused on our mission? By staying in God's Word. Just like that brownie coming out of the oven, delight yourself in the Word of God. Enjoy the aroma of Truth. Chew slowly and take it all in.

Challenge for today: Ask God for a passion for His Word. Block out time every day to read, study, and meditate on scripture. Hold it close to your heart, and let it fill your mind and soul. Let God's Word go deep and let it take over your life. Thank God today for His written Word and praise Him for the blessings of life.

Love Your Tailgater

I don't know about you, but there are two things that drive me crazy. The first is I hate to be lost. It drives me crazy not to know where I am going. Yes, I am one of those men who hate to ask for directions. If you want my family to be in an unhealthy family discussion, put us all in a car, and send us to a place we have never been. Most likely, I will make a wrong turn and tension will mount. The second thing the devil uses to get me off track is someone tailgating me. I know this shouldn't bother me, but it gets my blood pressure up. Don't you love it when someone is riding your bumper and they are in such a hurry, they finally zoom around you, and they are caught at the next red light? I would love to pull up beside them and wave and ask, "How is the tailgating working for you?" If the devil can't make me bad, he will send a tailgater on my bumper. Don't be surprised what the devil will use to trip you.

First Corinthians 16:13-14 says, "Be on your guard, stand firm in your faith; be men of courage; be strong. Do everything in love."

What tactic does Satan use on you? Be on your guard and keep your spiritual eyes open. Be aware of the spiritual battle that is going on around you daily.

Challenge for today: I encourage you to write down how the devil trips you. Then read through these two verses again, and see what God is telling you to do to counter his attack. God bless you today.

No Room?

What place does Jesus occupy in your heart? Have you ever stopped and asked yourself that question? Does he have the top priority, or have we given him a manager? Luke 2:7: "And she gave birth to her firstborn, a son. She wrapped him in clothes and placed him in a manger, because there was no room in the inn."

How many times have you heard those words from the Bible story? Have you ever asked the question, how could they do that to the baby Jesus? He deserved better. He deserved the best. The truth is, he deserved a whole lot better than a cattle stall and a feeding trough. But we tend to give him our second best and sometimes even our leftovers.

Jesus deserves the best room we have available. The fact is, most of the time we give him the less deserved things: How many times do we skip our Bible reading to scroll Facebook one more time? We choose to watch a movie over serving someone else.

Matthew 6:33: "But seek first His Kingdom and His righteousness, and all these things will be given to you as well."

This world has it all backwards. The world tells us to do "all the things" and fit God in where we can. If we make a commitment to live for God alone and daily revisit and live by our decision, we will do more of what really matters and less of what doesn't. Let's get our focus back to what really matters - Jesus.

Challenge for today: Slow down and take time to evaluate your commitments. List and rank those things you hold dear. Identify the areas where you are struggling? Make Jesus your greatest priority and give Him the most attention. He gave His best, so, we should return the favor.

Help a Brother Out

James 5:19-20: "My brothers, if one of you should wander from the truth and someone should bring him back, remember this; Whoever turns a sinner from the error of his ways will save him from death and cover over a multitude of sins."

We all go through a lot of the same stuff, but it just looks a little different in each of our lives. I encourage you to be willing to be real with other people and be open to share your own struggles and weaknesses. If you are like me, that goes against my nature. Don't be surprised how God can use you to encourage others when you share what God has taught you through your own struggles.

Do you have a friend who is struggling in their walk with God? Is there someone who is down and out? Ecclesiastes 4:9-12: "Two are better than one, because they have a good return for their work: If one falls down, his friends can help him up. But pity the man who falls and has no one to help him up! Also, if two lie together, they will keep warm. But how can one keep warm alone? Though one may be overpowered, two can defend themselves, a cord of three is not quickly broken."

We all need a word of encouragement and a helping hand sooner or later.

Challenge for today: Ask the Lord to open your spiritual eyes to the needs around you. Be open, be real, and share your story. Take time to encourage someone around you and look for opportunities to serve others. Always be ready to lend a helping hand.

Abram "The Man"

Genesis 12:1: "The Lord had said to Abram, "Leave your country, your people and your father's household and go to the land I will show you."

How hard would that be to leave everything we know to be obedient to Christ, especially when you don't know all the information. Back in my 20's, when we left for a trip, I would break out this huge map, and mark the best way to get to my destination. I would learn the names of each road and know exactly what turns to take. I would have my plan in place. Sometimes my plan wasn't as good as I thought. I don't know about you, but I hate getting lost.

Today it's much different, to say the least. I normally get an address, plug it in my phone, and I take off. Then I trust the GPS to get me there. Obedience is letting God set the direction of your life, even when he doesn't give us all the details. We must learn to follow Him step by step. God wants to align opportunity with obedience. God will give incredible opportunities to those who have learned to be obedient. Abram was that guy who stepped up to the plate and said, "Lord, I am your guy, what are we doing?" What is God calling you to do? What has God engraved in your heart? What has God set in motion in your life that you are trying your best to slow it down? What direction is God sending you but has not given you all the instructions and information?

Challenge for today: I challenge you to say to the Lord, "I am your guy, what are we doing?" The second part of my challenge is this easy, short prayer. Simply ask the Lord to give you an opportunity to serve Him. Then ask God for favor. Because of Abram's obedience, God not only blessed him, but He blessed an entire nation. What are you waiting on?

How Green Is Your Grass?

We seem to think that the grass is always greener on the other side of the fence. But we know that is not always true. How many times have we looked at other people's lives and thought, "They have it made." We look at other couples and think, "They have it all together." But things are not always as they seem. I want to share my thoughts with you and ask that you really pray about this. You see, the grass isn't always greener on the other side of the fence. It's greener where you water it. We must be willing to put in the work. James 1:19: "Know this, my beloved brothers: let every person be quick to hear, slow to speak, slow to anger."

One of the best pieces of marriage advice I ever received was this. Take plenty of time to listen and stop running your mouth. I encourage you to be intentional about how you "water." We need to be super intentional about how we invest in others and our close relationships. That may sound easy and fluffy, but it is not easy. Yes, greener grass looks good, but it requires work and it's not going to happen overnight. It takes cultivating, extra attention, sometimes even sweat, and tears.

Challenge for today: Go the extra mile, write a handwritten note of encouragement, take your wife on a fun date, or just smile and say hello. Invest in others and water every chance you get. It may cost you, but it is sure worth it. God bless you and your family.

God Things Come to Those Who Wait

Have you ever been given a vision of what God wants you to do, and you can't wait to see it come to pass? It's like waiting for Christmas, but 1,000 times more intensified. God calls you to wait. The Lord gives His prophet Habakkuk a word that I want to share with you. Habakkuk 2:2-3: "Write down the revelation and make it plain on tablets so that a herald may run with it. For the revelation awaits an appointed time; it speaks of the end and will not prove false. Though it lingers, wait for it; it will certainly come and will not delay."

I encourage you when God has put something on your heart or placed passion in your soul, write it down and date it. Make it plain and clear because you may need it down the road as a reminder. Though this vision or promise of God may linger, I urge you to wait for a green light. Don't settle for anything less, and don't give up. A true vision from God always requires patience. I don't know about you, but I hate waiting. Waiting on God is our job. Waiting is working but waiting works.

Challenge for today: As you wait, pray, and don't rush into a vision of God without all your instructions. Prayer will always help reveal what you do not know. Think about that. Pray for an opportunity to use your gift and passions for the glory of the Lord. Pray for God's favor. We do not need more money or more talent, but we need God's favor. Don't forget, favor doesn't force, it flows. There is an old saying that goes like this: Good things come to those who wait. I want to change it a little bit to say: God things come to those who wait.

Mary's Willingness to Obey

When it comes to the Christmas Story, Mary didn't play the lead role, but she had a huge part in it to say the least. Most Bible scholars think Mary was 16 years old when she gave birth to Jesus. Plus, she was not married. In Matthew 1:19, we read that her own fiancé didn't believe her story before the angel of the Lord appeared to him and told him the truth. He was about to break off the engagement. Can you imagine the talk around town? If that wasn't enough, Mary had to travel while she was in labor and give birth in a stable. Giving birth is never easy, but this truly added to the difficulty. Here are two truths we can take away from Mary's life:

1. No matter what others think about you, God doesn't look at your earthly resume to determine your spiritual worth. Thank goodness Mary's faith was stronger than the doubts in her mind and the gossip from the crowd.
2. If you decide to live boldly for Christ, it won't always be easy, but it will be worth it. Doing God's work will always have its challenges and will always have its rewards too. I love Mary's final words to the angel in Luke 1:38: "I am the Lord's servant. May your words to me be fulfilled."

Mary wasn't focused on the now, but she was focused on what she knew the Lord would do through obedience.

Challenge for today: Pray this prayer, "Lord help me to keep my focus on you. Don't let me get caught up in the approval of others. Use me in a way that you will receive glory."

Soaring Spiritually?

How is your spiritual life? In other words, how is your walk with God? Is your time with God vital or does God seem 1,000 miles away? When was the last time you stopped long enough to hear God's voice? For many of us, if we were to be honest, we are struggling, and we have been running on empty for a long time. We have been just going through the motions of doing church. You may be a professing Christian and go to church every Sunday, but you are not happy. You sure don't have joy in your life. Do you long to be victorious and passionate about your spiritual life again? At one time or another, we have all been there.

Victorious passionate Christian living is the result of knowing God for who He is. It's about standing humbly before the height of His holiness and amazed at the depth of His love. Then and only then, will you soar in your spiritual walk. If we can't escape the power of sin, depression, or defeat, it's not because our wills are weak, but it's because the presence of God feels so distant. We must enlarge our view of God. Embrace your Heavenly Father's eternal love for you. Soak in His presence. Rest in His grace and mercy. Worship and praise Him. Come near to God, and He will come near to you. James 3:6-8: "God opposes the proud but gives grace to the humble. Submit yourself, then to God. Resist the Devil, and he will flee from you. Come near to God and he will come near to you. Wash your hands, you sinners, and purify your hearts, you double minded."

Challenge for today: It's time for a change. It's time to grow. It's time to stop doing life your way and making life all about you. Humble yourself before Almighty God and get things right with Him. Let Him wash you clean, surrender your heart and life to Him. Stand in His holiness and soak in His presence. Then soar. His presence changes our atmosphere.

Something Worth Celebrating

In the United States of America, there are some very radical and crazy fans when it comes to football. Most people have never played a down of football in their life. But, somehow, they have become football experts. When I was young, I remember playing football from sunup to sundown. Yes, football is fun and exciting, but in the grand scheme of things, does it really matter? I would love to see my Georgia Bulldogs win another National Championship, but it won't change my life.

I want to share Isaiah 53:3-7: "He was despised and rejected by men, a man of sorrow, and familiar with suffering. Like one from whom men hide their faces he was despised, and we esteemed him not. Surely, he took up our infirmities and carried our sorrows, yet we considered him stricken by God, smitten by him, and afflicted. But he was pierced for our transgressions, he was crushed for our iniquities; the punishment that brought us peace was upon him, and by his wounds we are healed. We all like sheep, have gone astray, each of us has turned to his own way; and the Lord has laid on him the iniquity of us all. He was oppressed and afflicted, yet he didn't open his mouth; he was led like a lamb to the slaughter; as a sheep before her shearers is silent, so he did not open his mouth."

This scripture tells us of the great sacrifice that Jesus made for me and you. Think about how we take Jesus's love and grace for granted. How many days go by, and we never say thank you? How many times have we heard this preached or taught, and we sit there and not be overwhelmed? We get more passionate about a football game than we are about the God of the universe. Jesus willingly left the splendor of Heaven and laid down His life on a rugged cross, to save a sorry fellow like me. He took the punishment that I deserved. He overcame sin and death so I can experience true life and His amazing grace. Now that is worth cheering for. That is worth celebrating and this Truth will change your life. God bless and have a great time today.

Challenge for today: Celebrate what Christ has done for you. Thank Him out loud and take extra time to worship Him.

When Life Is Jacked Up?

Check out Luke 7:36-39 "Now one of the Pharisees invited Jesus to have dinner with him, so he went to the Pharisee's house and reclined at the table. When a woman who had lived a sinful life in that town learned that Jesus was eating at the Pharisee's house, she brought an alabaster jar of perfume, and as she stood behind him at his feet weeping, she began to wet his feet with her tears. Then she wiped them with her hair, kissed his feet and poured perfume on them. When the Pharisee who had invited him observed this, he said to himself, 'If this man were a prophet, he would know who is touching him and what kind of woman she is-that she is a sinner.'"

This woman had a lot of baggage. She had made some mistakes, but it didn't stop her from coming to Jesus. Remember it's not about what you are going through, but it's about who you are going to. This world loves to put labels on people, but God is in the business of changing your name and your heart. If you are broken, come to Jesus. If you are ashamed, come to Jesus. If you are depressed, come to Jesus. If you are addicted, come to Jesus. If your life is jacked up, come to Jesus. First John 5:4-5: "For everyone born of God overcomes the world. This is the victory that has overcome the world, even our faith. Who is it that overcomes the world? Only he who believes that Jesus is the Son of God."

No matter what you are facing, decide to come to Jesus.

Challenge for today: Lighten your load and drop your baggage at Jesus' feet. He is a God of grace, and He is standing with His arms wide open. Walk in freedom and experience the peace you can only find in a relationship with Jesus Christ.

God's Ultimate Intention

I want to take you back to the Old Testament, but first, thank God for three things. This will only take a few seconds, but it will change your entire day...your entire outlook. We need to be thankful 365 days a year. Let God hear your voice and let Him sense the gratitude of your heart.

Jeremiah 9:23-24: "This is what the Lord says: 'Let not the wise boast of his wisdom or the strong man boast of his strength or the rich man boast of his riches, but let him who boasts boast about this: that he understands and knows me, that I am the Lord, who exercises kindness, justice and righteousness on earth, for in these I delight,' declares the Lord."

What is God's ultimate intention for your life? I encourage you to slow down enough to really think about this question. God's ultimate intention for us is to know Him. It is not all about how much money we make or how strong we are, nor is it about how smart we have become. But His desire for us is to know Him and to enjoy His presence. This is what delights the Lord. This is what puts a smile on God's face. We were created for fellowship. We were created to worship the Lord. Stop chasing the things of this world that are leaving you empty and void. He is calling out to you. How will you respond?

Challenge for today: The things of this world will pass away. They don't last forever. Take time each day to get to know your Heavenly Father. Invest in the things that will last for all eternity. Begin with your relationship with Jesus. Make a commitment to increase your time alone with the Lord. It will be time well spent.

Stop And Reflect

I want to share a quick thought with you from my time alone with God. I must be honest with you, sometimes I want to hear that huge message from God that is going to radically change my life. I want it to be loud and obvious. How about you? But most of the time, God will speak a short and simple word that will cause you to sit and think. I want us to read a crazy little verse that is lingering in my heart.

Job 37:14: "Listen to this, Job; stop and consider God's wonders."

I should have moved on, but I kept reading it repeatedly. Then the Lord asked me a question, "Have you forgotten who I am and what I have done for you in the past?" I don't know about you, but sometimes I forget how big my God is. I get lost in my selfish pride and my earthly mindset. I tend to lean on my own understanding and reasoning. I shrink back and I forget about Who is really in control. Then I must step back and reflect.

Psalm 111:1-4: "Praise the Lord. I will extol the Lord with all my heart in the council of the upright and in the assembly. Great are the works of the Lord; they are pondered by all who delight in them. Glorious and majestic are his deeds and his righteousness endures forever. He caused his wonders to be remembered; the Lord is gracious and compassionate."

Challenge for today: Take time to stop and reflect on how faithful God is. Take time to slow down and praise God for who He is and how He has blessed you. Stop and consider His wonders.

Who Do We Turn To?

I love the Word of God. It is the source of encouragement in my life, and it seems God gives me just what I need at just the right time. I want to share a gift with you today, and I pray that it encourages you.

Psalm 121:1-8: "I lift my eyes to the hills-where does my help come from? My help comes from the Lord, the maker of heaven and earth. He will not let your foot slip-He who watches over you will not slumber; indeed, He who watches over Israel will neither slumber nor sleep. The Lord watches over you-the Lord is your shade at your right hand; the sun will not harm you by day, nor the moon by night. The Lord will keep you from all harm-He will watch over your life; the Lord will watch over your coming and going both now and forevermore."

Our help comes from the Lord, and we need to trust Him. We must remind ourselves that God didn't save Daniel from the Lion's Den, but He saved him IN the Lion's Den. God doesn't get us out, but He does get us through. Psalm 125:1: "Those who trust in the Lord are like Mount Zion, which cannot be shaken but endures forever!"

Put your faith and trust in a God who never sleeps, because He has His eyes on you. You are adored by the God of the universe, and He has an awesome plan for your life. Hang on; don't give up. God has your back.

Challenge for today: Write a letter to the Lord. Yes, get a piece of paper and a pen and tell Him all the things that are causing you stress and grief. Pour your heart out to the Lord and ask Him to give you peace and comfort. Know this, He cares for you greatly, and He loves you with a never-ending love. Turn to the One who will always be there for you.

Fresh Look

As we look at Luke 7:1-10, I pray that God's Word will come alive in your heart. Don't be hesitant to dig deeper. In the story of the centurion and his great faith, there is an obvious truth. But if we keep digging, we will find another truth that will hit home. The Jews in Jesus' day knew that only one person had ultimate authority over nature: God. God spoke creation into existence. In Luke 7:7 the centurion said, "Say the word, and my servant will be healed."

By claiming that Jesus could control the natural world by merely speaking, the centurion associated Jesus with the all-powerful Creator God. At Jesus' word, just like God, creation would obey.

Luke 7:9: "When Jesus heard this, he was amazed at him."

Wow, did you catch that? Jesus, the Son of God, the Savior of my soul, the second person of the Trinity, was amazed. He was amazed at great faith. The centurion placed his faith in Jesus, and he confessed that all he needed was Jesus to speak, and his servant would be healed. In scripture, two things amazed Jesus:

1. Great faith.
2. Lack of faith.

When Jesus looks at your life, what does He see? Does your life amaze Jesus? Just something to think about today.

Challenge for today: Ask yourself these questions, what am I doing that needs the power of God to get accomplished? Dare to dream a God dream. What has God placed in your heart? What is your greatest dream for your life and ministry? Now multiply it by twenty. That would be your God dream. We are all guilty of dreaming too small.

A Fresher Look

I want to challenge you to read Luke 7:1-10 again. I have read this scripture so many times before, and I have prepared lessons and sermons using this passage. The one thing that has always stood out was the faith of the centurion. But I want to share another thought that blew me away. You know how the story goes: the centurion had requested to send elders to go to Jesus and ask him to come and heal the centurion's beloved servant. The servant was very sick and about to die. Jesus agreed to go with the elders to heal the centurion's servant. But before Jesus reached the centurion home, the centurion sent some friends to tell Jesus not to come. What was going on in the centurion's head? He just sent elders to get Jesus, and now he is sending friends to tell Jesus not to come. I believe the centurion knew he needed Jesus' help, but he also knew he didn't deserve his help.

The closer Jesus gets to us, the more we realize just how far away we are from him. When the centurion realized Jesus was getting closer, he panicked. He begins to think: What if he comes inside? What if Jesus sees the mess my house is in? What if he sees the real me? It's sad, but many people think about Jesus this way. Jesus wants to come to their home, but when he gets closer, they get nervous and send him away. We all have been through some tough times. There have been moments where we have made some bad decisions, and times when we have sinned against God. But through it all, your value has never changed. You are priceless in His eyes, and you are so loved by Him. You may feel unworthy, but He is trying to get to you. Your house may be in a mess, but don't push Him away. This passage talks about the centurion's faith but it's really all about Jesus.

Challenge for today: Don't push Jesus away. As you grow closer to Christ, He will begin to reveal your true heart and expose your motives. Welcome that truth in your life. We need more of Him and less of us. Tell your Father, "I welcome your presence. Clean me up, God, and make me more like you." I dare you.

What's Your Escape Route

Most of us try to resist temptation, and that is why we lose repeatedly. When we try to resist in the flesh, we will lose because the flesh wants to give in. The flesh is what got you in the situation with this temptation in the first place. In Matthew 26:41 Jesus said to his disciples: "Watch and pray so that you don't fall into temptation. The spirit is willing, but the flesh is weak."

How true is that? Paul writes in Galatians 5:16-17: "Live by the Spirit, and you will not gratify the desires of the sinful nature. For the sinful nature desires what is contrary to the Spirit, and the Spirit is contrary to the sinful nature. They conflict with each other, so that you do not do what you want." It's a battle at times to say the least.

Instead of trying to resist temptation, I encourage you to turn and run away. Second Timothy 2:22: "Flee the evil desires of youth, and pursue righteousness, faith, love and peace, along with those who call on the Lord out of a pure heart."

How can you break the pull of temptation if you don't run from it? Renowned author, Peter Lord, uses a great example that I want to share with you. He said, "Temptation is like a magnet field. If a piece of iron is brought inside the magnetic field, the iron will be pulled and attracted to the magnet. But if you keep the iron outside the magnetic field, the iron will not be pulled in because it is outside the field's sphere of influence. Forbidden fruit also has a magnetic field. When you stay away from the object of temptation, you are outside the sphere of influence, and you will not feel the magnet pull toward it."

First Corinthians 10:13: "No temptation has seized you except what is common to man. And God is faithful, he will not let you be tempted beyond what you can bear. But when you are tempted, he will provide the way out so that you can stand under it."

Challenge for today: God will always make a way out of temptation, but we must look for it. Recognize how Satan tripped you last time. He loves to use the same old tricks repeatedly. Beware of your surroundings and know that temptation is coming. When it comes, look for a way to escape.

On Your Feet

Thank the Lord for His patience and His amazing love.

Psalm 100:1-5: "Shout for joy to the Lord, all the earth. Worship the Lord with gladness; come before him with joyful songs. Know that the Lord is God. It is he who made us, and we are his; we are his people, the sheep of his pasture. Enter his gates with thanksgiving and his courts with praise; give thanks to him and praise his name. For the Lord is good and his love endures forever; his faithfulness continues through all generations."

God is good and God is for me. On your feet Church, applaud the living God for He is worthy. Take time to take a snapshot of that in your mind. Bring a gift of laughter. Sing yourself into the presence of God. Thank Him and worship Him. Don't forget Who our Creator is. He made us; we didn't make Him. Enter His presence with the password: "Thank you."

I urge you in the business of your day, make sure to take the time to bow your head, and give thanks. Psalm 103:1-5: "Praise the Lord, O my soul; all my inmost being, praise his holy name. Praise the Lord, O my soul, and forget not all his benefits, who forgives all your sins and heals all our diseases, who redeems your life from the pit and crowns you with love and compassion, who satisfies your desires with good things!"

On your feet and thank Him. On your feet and praise Him. May God bless you and keep you safe today.

Challenge for today: This may sound strange, but I want you to stand up and clap for the God of the universe. Then I want you to shout praise to Him. Don't hesitate, just do it. Reflect on God's goodness and see all the blessings that flow from His hands. On your feet Church. Give Him what He deserves. Give Him some praise.

Don't You Dare

How many times do you put on a mask and pretend everything is great in your lives? But you are dying on the inside, you are overwhelmed, and you are at the end of your rope. Maybe you have lost someone that you loved so much, and you are hurting inside. Maybe you have a child that is on the wrong road, and you are sick and tired of them wasting away. You may be struggling financially, and you see no way out. Maybe you just found out you have cancer. We have all been there, so don't feel alone. It's hard, but it's not impossible to overcome.

I want to share a verse with you today. Luke 18:1: "Jesus told his disciples a parable to show them that they should pray and not give up."

If you are struggling to find a smile or looking for the light at the end of the tunnel, there is hope. Don't you dare give up, keep on praying. God is always working behind the scenes, and most of the time we don't see it. Just know that He is still in the miracle working business. Never forget; "Greater is He that is in you, then he that is in the world."

Hold on to this truth, keep on praying, keep on loving, and don't give up. God has your back.

Challenge for today: Ask God for peace, joy, and wisdom. Stop acting like nothing is wrong and take the mask off that you are wearing. It is ok to grieve, and you don't always have to wear a smile. But don't give up. Don't roll over. Keep on praying and keep on believing. I pray for your encouragement, and I pray that you trust the God of heaven and earth to watch over you. Keep the faith.

Living for Self

We are so blessed, and we need to be thankful for all the blessings of God. Lift a prayer of praise today.

James 3:14-16: "But if you harbor bitter envy and selfish ambition in your heart, do not boast about it or deny the truth. Such 'wisdom' does not come down from heaven but is earthly, unspiritual, of the devil. For where you have envy and selfish ambition, there you find disorder and every evil practice."

I can only speak for myself; I am by nature a very selfish person. We ask questions like: "What's in it for me? How is this going to benefit me and my family? How can I get ahead?" We want to make it all about us. Selfish living will hinder your ability to bless others. Proverbs 11:25: "A generous man will prosper; he who refreshes others will himself be refreshed."

God is calling us away from our selfish nature, and is encouraging us to serve, and to love the people around us. Luke 6:38: "Give and it will be given to you. A good measure, pressed down, shaken together and running over, will be poured into your lap. For with the measure you use, it will be measured to you."

"I hear you, Lord."

Challenge for today: Pray over Galatians 2:20 and see what the Lord is telling you. Galatians 2:20: "I have been crucified with Christ and I no longer live, but Christ lives in me. The life I live in the body, I live by faith in the Son of God, who loved me and gave himself for me."

I dare you to pray this repeatedly to your Heavenly Father. I double dog dare you. Who are you living for?

He's Big

After David defeated Goliath, he stopped to write Psalm 8:1-3. I am sure he was overwhelmed with the power of God and the strength he received from the Heavenly Father. Think about it, David's faith put him in a position where he had to put his trust in someone bigger than himself. He experienced victory over an undefeated killing machine, and it was due to God's power. I am sure when the adrenaline wore off, David asked himself, "What just happened?"

Psalm 8:1-3: "O Lord, our Lord, how majestic is Your name in all the earth. You have set Your glory above the heavens. From the lips of children and infants You have ordained praise because of your enemies, to silence the foe and the avenger. When I consider Your heavens, the work of Your fingers, the moon and the stars, which You have set in place, what is man that You are mindful of him, the son of man that You care for him."

Lord, you are bigger than I thought you were, and it's hard to imagine how big You really are. Our God is all powerful and all knowing. He is the very Creator of heaven and earth. He spoke everything into existence. He is the Alpha and the Omega, the beginning and the end. He is my rock, my fortress, and my Deliverer. He is my shield, my stronghold, and He is Lord. If God is for me, who can stand against me? Church, don't back down and never waver in fear but put your trust in a huge and powerful God that loves you.

Challenge for today: Ask yourself:
1. How big is the God I serve?
2. Do I live a life of faith and trust God to watch over me?
3. What is your power source that keeps you going and full of faith?
4. Do you even need God to accomplish your dreams?
5. What is God asking of you today?

Dream big because we serve a BIG God.

Perfect Timing

I want to unload some truth to your front door. My heart's desire is to share the Word of God and encourage those around me. Honestly, I enjoy writing devotions, it gives me an outlet to share what God has been placing on my heart. I want to be found faithful and do what God has called me to do. He can take our small, inadequate talent and turn it into something God-sized. That's my God!

Romans 5:6-8: "You see, at just the right time, when we were still powerless, Christ died for the ungodly. Very rarely will anyone die for a righteous man, though for a good man someone might possibly dare to die. But God demonstrates his own love for us in this: While we were still sinners, Christ died for us."

At just the right time. Whether we want to believe it or not, God has a master plan, and He has it all figured out. How many times do we get frustrated with God when things don't go as we think they should? Sometimes God's timing doesn't make sense, but that is when we need to trust Him. How hard is it to trust Him? I encourage you to say this repeatedly throughout the day: At just the right time. At just the right time. Just a reminder that He loves you and has an awesome plan for your life. Be faithful and wait on His perfect timing.

Challenge for today: Know in your heart that God has your best interest in mind. Know that He is going before you and preparing the way. Be willing to follow His plan and seek His presence. Say, "At just the right time," over and over today as a reminder that God is faithful. Wear a rubber band around your wrist and write on it: At just the right time. Stay focused on truth that will encourage you, not the problems at hand.

Get An Attitude

God is good and He is good all the time. Amen.

I want to share Philippians 2:1-4: "If you have any encouragement from being united with Christ, if any comfort from his love, if any fellowship with the Spirit, if any tenderness and compassion, then make my joy complete by being like-minded, having the same love, being one in spirit and purpose. Do nothing out of selfish ambition or vain conceit, but in humility consider others better than yourselves. Each of you should look not only to your own interest, but also to the interest of others."

I encourage you to imitate Christ in all you do. But to imitate Christ we need to:
1. Maximize our view of God and who He is. He is the all-knowing, powerful Creator of the world, and He cares about me.
2. We need to recognize the needs of people around us and be willing to do something about it.
3. We need to minimize attention to ourselves. I don't know about you, but I can be very selfish at times.

Read on with me, Philippians 2:5-8: "Your attitude should be the same as that of Jesus Christ: Who being in the very nature God, did not consider equality with God something to be grasped, but made himself nothing, taking the very nature of a servant, being made in human likeness. And being found in appearance as a man, he humbled himself and became obedient to death-even death on a cross."

Challenge for today: Pray for the attitude of Christ. Keep your gaze on the Father, see the needs around you, and die to self-daily. Get an attitude, the attitude of Christ. Again, God is good, and He is good all the time.

There Is No Time Like Today

I want to open with two verses today. Hebrews 3:7: "Today, if you hear his voice, do not harden your hearts."

Hebrews 3:13 says, "But encourage one another daily, as long as it is called today."

I am not talking about yesterday and what happened in the past, and I am not talking about the future and the possibility that is in front of us. There is nothing wrong with learning from our past or being excited about what God has in our near future. But we must make the most of what God has for us today. We need to make today count for the Glory of Christ.

We are not promised tomorrow. Life is a precious gift that is given by God, and we don't need to take that for granted. I have lost a couple of students to death. Yes, it seems so unfair, and it broke our hearts. We must know that we all have an hourglass in our life, and when we take our first breath God turns that hourglass over. Then the sands of life begin to run, and when our sand runs out, our time on earth is done. There is no time like today.

Challenge for today: Encourage three people with a simple act of kindness. Pay for someone's lunch. Call an old friend to say you love them. Share your faith with someone without Christ. Spend extra time in prayer listening at your Father's feet. Make a difference in someone's life. Let's put our faith to work. Don't look past the opportunities that God puts in front of us today. We are not guaranteed tomorrow but we do have today. There is no time like TODAY!

Four Things

Praise the God of heaven and earth. Proverbs 2:1-5: "My son, if you accept my words and store up my commands within you, turning your ears to wisdom and applying your heart for understanding, and if you call out for insight and cry aloud for understanding, and if you look for silver and search it as for hidden treasure, then you will understand the fear of the Lord and find the knowledge of God."

God's Word is laying down a solid foundation for us and is giving us spiritual food to feast on today. Notice the word 'if'. It is mentioned three times in this scripture. In other words, we have a choice to obey God's Word, or not. There are four things we need to understand to fear the Lord and to walk in wisdom.

First, we need to be teachable. We need to learn how to listen a whole lot better and make it a priority to learn Truth.

Second, we need to be willing to be obedient to what the Lord teaches us. We need to know how to apply the Truth to everyday life.

Third, we need to be dependent on prayer. When will we learn to truly trust Him and to lean on our Heavenly Father? If it is on your heart, or weighing you down, take the time to talk it out with your Heavenly Father. Share your concerns and worries and take time to hear what He is saying to you.

Fourth, we need to understand perseverance. We need to keep on, keeping on. There will be trials along the way, and there will be obstacles that will slow us down. But keep your eyes on the prize of knowing Christ. Keep pushing forward, and don't look back.

Challenge for today: Be teachable, obedient, dependent on prayer, and persevere in your walk with Christ. Then you will understand the fear of the Lord and find the knowledge of God. Follow the map, and you will find the treasure.

Serving Others

Take three steps that will change tomorrow.

1. Make yourself available.

Matthew 25:38-40: "When did we see you a stranger and invite you in, or needing clothes and clothe you? When did we see you sick or in prison and go and visit you?" The King will reply, 'I tell you the truth, whatever you did for the least of these brothers of mine, you did for me.'"

When we serve others, we serve God. The number one ingredient to serving is availability. We need to be present in people's lives. But the greatest enemy of availability is busyness. If Satan can't make you bad, he will make you busy.

2. Meet the needs of people around you.

First Peter 4:10: "Each one should use whatever gift he has received to serve others, faithfully administering God's Grace in its various forms."

God has gifted each follower of Christ with a gift, and that gift was given to us to encourage others. The Church is the only organization that exists for those outside of their organization. Mark 10:45: "For even the Son of Man didn't come to be served, but to serve, and to give his life as a ransom for many."

3. Move people toward Jesus.

Our job is not to be this world's savior; our job is to point them to Jesus. He is their hope and Savior. Our job isn't to pull people out of sin and darkness, but to point them to Jesus. John the Baptist was a great example. He was the forerunner of Christ. He wasn't the answer for sin, guilt, and shame. Everything he did pointed others to Christ.

Challenge for today: Serve the Lord with all your heart by serving others. Use this strategy to make sure we are loving others the way that Jesus loved. Make yourself available. Meet the needs of people around you. Move others to Christ.

Waiting on the Call

It's a new day and there is no doubt that God is alive, active, and wanting to speak to us daily. God speaks to us in various ways. He speaks through impressions, dreams, the Word of God, and godly friends. If we are in Christ, He has a specific mission for us and He will take His time to prepare us for it. Most of the time, waiting is involved. Waiting will bring clarity. Waiting will bring passion. Take time to read First Samuel 3:1-11. There is so much truth in these few verses, but I can only scrap a little bit off in this devotion. Here are four things to do while waiting on a call.

1. Choose to get under before you get over.

In other words, get under a godly leader that God has placed over you. Take time to learn, receive instructions and wisdom. The boy Samuel ministered before the Lord under Eli. Great things come wrapped up with obstacles. We all need someone with wisdom to guide us and direct us.

2. Align yourself with God.

Notice in First Samuel 3:2, Eli was lying in his usual place. He was doing the same ole, same ole. He was toward the end of his life, and he was in a spiritual rut. But verse three tells us this, "The lamp of God had not gone out, and Samuel was lying down in the temple of the Lord, where the ark of God was."

The ark of the covenant represents God's presence. Samuel wanted to be as close as he could be to the presence of God. Are you positioned to have an interruption from God? An alignment with God creates an assignment from God.

3. Lie in your place.

Can we be content if God doesn't give us anything else? Will we be ok if God doesn't give us this huge assignment? Samuel wasn't looking for a calling, but the calling was looking for him. Be in your place and serve faithfully. Be content where God has you.

4. Listen carefully.

Notice in verses four through ten, the Lord called to Samuel repeatedly. Each time Samuel got up and went to Eli. In First Samuel 3:8, Eli finally told Samuel, "The Lord is calling to you. Go and lie down, and when He calls, tell him to speak."

Sure enough, God called out to Samuel again. First Samuel 3:10: "Samuel answered and said, 'Speak, for your servant is listening.'"

Samuel had the right intention but the wrong direction. Spend time, without distractions. Listen to the Lord.

Challenge for today: Choose to be under godly leadership. Align yourself with the Lord. Lie in your place. Listen carefully. Waiting brings clarity.

Stay In Your Lane

How many of us hate driving on two lane country roads at night especially when it is raining so hard one can barely see the road? It gets worse when the oncoming traffic doesn't take their bright lights off. (That is almost as bad as people riding five feet from your bumper. You think I am kidding...that is when I must pray the most. I am dead serious. My old self comes out and I need intervention from the Lord.) On that two-lane road at night, I must keep my eyes on that white running line to my right. My thought process is to just stay in my lane, and I will make it home.

This made me think about Proverbs 4:23-27: "Above all else, guard your heart, for it is the wellspring of life. Put away perversity from the mouth; keep corrupt talk from your lips. Let your eyes look straight ahead, fix your gaze directly before you. Make level paths for your feet and take only ways that are firm. Do not swerve to the right or the left; keep your foot from evil."

We must look straight ahead and look for that white running line which is Jesus Christ. Satan will do everything he can to distract you, blur your vision, and cause you to look away.

Are your eyes wondering? Have you lost focus? Has your heart fallen for other gods? Things like sports, money, power, or position can be those gods. These things will leave you in a ditch and crying out for help.

Challenge for today: Guard your heart and what you say. Keep your focus on what is most important and keep Christ first in your life. Don't swerve to the left or right and stay away from the tricks of the devil. Stay in your lane bro.

Try This

There is nothing more powerful than praying scripture. If you don't believe me, then try it for yourselves. I want to share a scripture, and then I encourage you to pray through it with the Lord. Have a conversation with Him about what you just prayed. You will never be the same.

Psalm 119:33-40: "Teach me, O Lord, to follow your decrees; then I will keep them to the end. Give me understanding, and I will keep your law and obey it with all my heart. Direct me in the path of your commands, for there I find delight. Turn my heart towards your statutes and not toward selfish gain. Turn my eyes away from worthless things; preserve my life according to your word. Fulfill your promises to your servant, so that you may be feared. Take away the disgrace I dread, for your laws are good. How I long for your precepts! Preserve my life in righteousness."

Yes, Lord. This is the truth that will change your heart and give you a whole new perspective for life. Take time to meditate on His Word, and let it go deep. Stop skimming over the Bible and trying to cover so many chapters a day. Take time to enjoy the richness of God's written Word and apply this truth to your life and savor His relationship.

Challenge for today: After you pray through this scripture, allow God time to speak to you. Don't be in a rush and don't be scared to ask Him questions. Now write down what He told you or impressed on your heart. Kick some dents in the gates of Hell today.

Don't Lose Heart

Second Corinthians 4:16-18: "Therefore we do not lose heart. Though outwardly we are wasting away, yet inwardly we are being renewed day by day. For our light and momentary troubles are achieving for us an eternal glory that far outweighs them all. So, we fix our eyes not on what is seen, but what is unseen. For what is seen is temporary, but what is unseen is eternal."

So many times, in life we stop and look at all the negative, and evil things going on in our world. It can be overwhelming and discouraging. Murder of unborn babies is happening every day. Lives are being destroyed by drugs and alcohol ripping families apart. Human trafficking of children has become a money-making business. Are you kidding me? Divorce is rampant not only in the world but in the church as well. Families are being destroyed by selfishness and greed. Pornography is off the charts; it is destroying the mind and heart of mankind. Men and women are confused when it comes to a relationship with each other. All these things can be super discouraging and frustrating to say the least.

Paul is telling us not to lose heart but to be renewed day by day. He is encouraging us to turn our eyes towards Jesus and to grow in our love relationship with Him. We need to be fueled by the Savior of the world. We need to be filled by the Holy Spirit of God. We need to be empowered by the God of the universe. Paul tells us in Galatians 6:9: "Let us not become weary in doing good, for at the proper time we will reap a harvest if we do not give up."

Let this truth sink in.

Challenge for today: I encourage you to believe in God for the impossible, to grow in your relationship with Christ, and God will show you what to do about the world around you. What are you fixed on? The troubles of this world or Jesus? Don't lose heart, Church, but be super charged by our Creator.

Where Do You Run?

David was a hero of the faith and a great king. He never claimed to be perfect, but he pursued God with passion. David also had many enemies who wanted his head on a platter, but David trusted in the Lord, his Deliverer. David wrote a song to the Lord in Psalm 18:1-2: "I love you, O Lord, my strength. The Lord is my Rock, my Fortress and my Deliverer; my God is my rock, in whom I take refuge. He is my shield and my horn of my salvation, my stronghold."

How did David withstand all the pressures of this life and face his stressful job? If you think you have a ton on your plate, try being king. His secret was found in his relationship with God. David wrote Psalm 27:1-3: "The Lord is my light and my salvation-whom shall I fear? The Lord is my stronghold of my life-of whom shall I be afraid? When evil men advance against me to devour my flesh, when my enemies and my foes attack me, they will stumble and fall. Though an army besiege me, my heart will not fear; though war breaks out against me, even then I will be confident."

David's time with God was his stronghold, and his high tower. Here is where he found his strength and confidence to do what he was called to. We all need a high tower and a shelter when the storms of life come.

Challenge for today: Run to the One who loves you the most, and He will welcome you with open arms no matter what. Thank the Lord for watching over you and loving you so freely. Give Him the praise and the glory that He deserves. He is your rock, your shelter, and your comfort. To Him be the Glory forever and ever.

This Is for You

I encourage you to stop and thank God for five things. Thank Him out loud, and even write it on a piece of paper. Place that paper where you can see it throughout the day. It is refreshing to see a reminder of how blessed we really are. Then think about ways you could express your gratitude to the Lord for your many blessings.

Another challenge is to think of three people that have invested in you over the years. It could be someone that has loved you through the thick and the thin. Maybe it's someone who has gone out of their way to encourage and mold you. Then give them a call and say thank you. Notice I didn't say to send them a text.

Let's give thanks to the Lord for his unfailing love and wonderful deeds for men, for he satisfies and fills the hungry with good things. Let the world know how good our God is. "Thank you, Lord, for the blessing of life that we have through the blood of Jesus Christ. Amen." Let's go Church! This is the day that the Lord has made; let us be thankful and celebrate it all day long.

Psalm 105:1-4: "Give thanks to the Lord, call on his name; make known among the nations what he has done. Sing to him, sing praise to him; tell of all his wonderful acts. Glory in his holy name; let the hearts of those who seek the Lord rejoice. Look to the Lord and his strength; seek his face always."

Challenge for today: Find two other verses with praise and thankfulness. Write these verses down and commit them to memory. Make a commitment to the Lord that you will daily have a time of praise and thanksgiving. When you begin to complain or be negative, go back to these scriptures and read them over again. Express your heart of gratitude daily.

A Prayer That Helps Me to Stay on Track

I am not sure what I would do without God's Word. Let me tell you, it is so easy to get off track and then get stuck in a rut. God prepared His Holy Scriptures for situations just like this. He knew we would need instruction and encouragement. He is our perfect Father.

Psalm 119:33-37: "Teach me, O Lord, to follow your decrees; then I will keep them to the end. Give me understanding, and I will keep your law and obey it with all my heart. Direct me in the path of your commands, for there I find delight. Turn my heart toward your statutes and not toward selfish gains. Turn my eyes away from worthless things; persevere in my life according to your word."

There will always be distractions and temptations that the devil throws in our path. He never gives up and he never seems to take it easy on us. He is determined to cause as much havoc in our lives as possible. But God has given us everything we need to be victorious and to overcome the traps of Satan. We don't have to walk in defeat and depression. Pray His Word and walk it out.

Challenge for today: For encouragement, use this scripture as a prayer to your Heavenly Father. Ask Him to teach you His ways, and to give you understanding. Pray that He will direct your path in every situation. Ask Him to guard your heart and turn your efforts and passions toward eternal things. It is a powerful thing when we learn how to pray through His scriptures. Lord, preserve my life in your righteousness and help me to stay on track. God bless you today.

Don't You Love This

I have a thought I want to share with you. I pray that it will encourage you but also motivate you. Philippians 2:9-11: "Therefore God exalted him to the highest place and gave him the name that is above every name, that every knee should bow, in heaven and in the earth, and under the earth, that every tongue confess that Jesus Christ is Lord, to the glory of God the Father." Amen.

There is coming a day when every tongue will confess that Jesus is Lord. It will be seen and heard here on earth, and in heaven, and even in Hell. Think about this, Satan will finally bow his head and admit it, "Jesus is Lord." Man, don't you love that. What a day that will be! Yes, there is power in the name of Jesus. First Corinthians 15:55-57: "Where, O death, is your victory? Where, O death, is your sting? The sting of death is sin, and the power of sin is the law. But thanks be to God! He gives us the victory through our Lord Jesus Christ!"

Shout from the rooftops that Jesus is Lord.

Revelation 21:4-7: "He will wipe every tear from their eyes. There will be no more death or mourning or crying or pain, for the old order of things has passed away. He who was seated on the throne said, 'I am making everything new!' Then he said, 'Write this down, for these words are trustworthy and true.' He said to me: 'It is done. I am the Alpha and the Omega, the Beginning and the End. To him who is thirsty I will give to drink without cost from the spring of the water of life, He who overcomes will inherit all this, and I will be his God and he will be my son.'"

Challenge for today: This may be strange, but just humor me. Say out loud seven times, "Jesus is Lord." Let this world know about the God you serve. Lift His name up in all you do.

I Am Guilty

Don't you love it when God gives you something that you need even though you may not want it. I want to share with you the scripture that God gave me that convicted me, and I had to stop and tell Him, "I am guilty."

Philippians 2:12-15: "My dear friends, as you have always obeyed-not only in my presence, but now much more in my absence-continue to work out your salvation with fear and trembling. For it is God who works in you to will and to act according to his good purpose. Do everything without complaining or arguing, so that you may become blameless and pure, children of God without fault in a crooked and depraved generation."

Have you ever found yourself in a season of complaining or arguing? It is so easy to get stuck there, but God is calling us to move from that spot. It's so easy to be critical, and when things are not going our way, we tend to complain. Is your work making you frustrated? Are your kids driving you up the wall? Is your car always messing up? My natural response is to complain, and I know I am guilty. What about you?

It's hard to always be positive and encouraging in a very critical and negative world, but God has called us to a higher standard. He has given us everything we need to be positive in negative situations. Hebrews 13:20-21: "May the God of peace, who through the blood of the eternal covenant brought back from the dead our Lord Jesus, that great Shepherd of the sheep, equip you with every good for doing his will, and may he work in us what is pleasing to him, through Jesus Christ, to whom be glory forever and ever."

God is working in you, giving you a desire and power to do what pleases Him.

Challenge for today: Take your eyes off self and place them on your Heavenly Father. Ask Him to change your heart and give you a fresh perspective on life. Stay prayed up and continue to work out your salvation with fear and trembling. I don't know about you, but I am a work in progress. Stay positive.

Where's The Passion?

It is amazing to see how so many can be so passionate about football. That is all they think about during the week. They get all decked out in their outfits, decorate their cars, fly their flags, and they even get a tattoo in some cases. They are passionate about their team. How many times have we found ourselves yelling at the TV, like they were going to hear us? I love to see people who are passionate and stand by their teams no matter what.

There was a great commercial aired years ago that featured three older ladies. It was a Wendy's commercial where three ladies were looking at a hamburger, huge bun and a very small piece of meat. A famous line was birthed that day when one of them said, "Where's the beef?" I want to use that slogan today, but I want to change one word. Where's the passion? Church, what consumes our thoughts? What motivates us? What do we dream about? What gets us excited? Where is our passion for God and the things of God? We have the opportunity every day to sit at the Father's feet and feast on the goodness of God. He has prepared a spiritual buffet table for us to dine in sweet fellowship. So many times, we walk away and eat our old spiritual bologna sandwich. Where is our passion? I want to give you three things that will help you to raise your passion level to an all-time high.

First, prayer must be a priority. This is where passion is birthed. We must have a continual conversation with our Heavenly Father. John 16:24: "Until now, you have not asked for anything in my name. Ask and you will receive, and your joy will be complete." Tell God exactly where you are. Be real. Then ask Him to give you that passion for Him like never before. Pray it, mean it, and believe it. "Lord, light a fire under Your Church."

Second, our priorities must be in line. Matthew 6:33: "But seek first his kingdom and his righteousness, and all these things will be given to you."

Why is worry and stress so evident in our society today? Why does everybody always seem to be worn out and tired? It's because we are chasing after the things of this world more than we chase after the things of God. Many families are in debt up to their eyeballs. We want the big truck, the nice house, and all the fancy vacations while God takes a back seat. It is so easy to lose our focus on what is most important. Trust me, I know. It's time to rearrange our priorities and put God where He belongs.

Last, but not least, if we are going to raise our passion level, we must be willing to give God everything. Yes, I am talking about total surrender. Matthew 16:24: "If anyone would come after me, he must deny himself and take up his cross and follow me." I know that isn't easy for us, but neither was dying on a cross. He willingly laid down His life on an old wooden cross. God deserves our best. Passion for God is found in fervent prayer. It's found in putting God first, and it is found in a total surrendered life.

Challenge for today: Spiritual contentment must go. The world is not screaming "where's the beef", but they are screaming "Where is the love? Where is the grace? Where is this Jesus?" I pray for you to seek passion.

The Peace of God

I pray today that you wake up with a smile on your face and an excitement in your soul because we GET to worship the God of the universe. God is good, and He is good all the time.

God's Word is a guide and a gift that the Holy Spirit has given us. It is full of truth and treasures that we need to live our lives. It also reveals God's heart, will, and purpose for His children. Listen to Philippians 4:4-7: "Rejoice in the Lord always. I will say it again: Rejoice! Let your gentleness be evident to all. The Lord is near. Do not be anxious about anything, but in everything, by prayer and petition, with thanksgiving, present your request to God. And the peace of God, which transcends all understanding, will guard your hearts and your minds in Christ Jesus."

In this life there are always difficulties, frustrations, and hard times. I wish that wasn't true, but we all face these times in life. Yet, His Word tells us to rejoice in the Lord always. As difficult as that sounds, during those hard times, know that the Lord is right there with you. Come near to God, and he will come near to you. He will give you the strength, courage, endurance, and the hope you need to keep going. Amp up your prayer life. In every situation in life, take it before the King and cover it in prayer. Tell God what you are dealing with and what is on your mind. Ask for wisdom and discernment in every situation.

Do you need His peace today? Are there things in your life that are causing you stress or grief? Lay it all at His feet today and trust Him with it. Be honest and stop pretending that you have it all under control. Hand it over to the Lord.

Challenge for today: Be thankful and praise Him for the smallest blessings. Then take time to present your burdens, troubles, and your worries to your Heavenly Father. Trust Him with it all. We serve a huge and powerful God. "Lord, give us a peace that can only come through you. Amen."

Lost/Carnal/Spiritual-Filled

I want to talk about three types of people. We are all in one of the three categories. In which category do you find yourself?

1. Lost:

He is dead at the center of his being. He is shaped by his environment. He is empty and looking for something to fill the void. He is under the control of 'self'. He has no hope and no peace.

2. Carnal:

He has come alive inside and Jesus has come to dwell in him. He is weak and still subject to outside influences. He is still shaped by his world or his peer group. He is attacked by Satan and has little defense. He has trouble with priorities. He is a fragmented person, trying to make the best of both worlds.

3. Spirit-filled:

He has affected a total sell out to Christ. He has died to 'self'. He has taken up the fact of his death and lives with it daily. He takes on Satan's attacks and is not overcome. He has an inner strength that helps him live out his life with boldness. He has enthroned Christ in his life and now Christ presides over his entire personality. The residing Christ becomes the presiding Christ. The resident Christ becomes the reigning Christ.

Challenge for today: Take that next step. God's desire for all of us is to grow in our relationship with Him, not to sit still or be content where we are in our walk with the Father. Don't get comfortable and lazy. He is calling out to you. What is that next step for you? Ask Him to make it clear and give you the guts to move forward. You got this.

Investing

Second Chronicles 1:7-10: "That night God appeared to Solomon and said to him, 'Ask anything you want me to give you.' Solomon answered God, 'You have shown me great kindness to David my father and have made me king in his place. Now, Lord God, let your promise to my father David be confirmed, for you have made me king over a people who are as numerous as the dust of the earth. Give me wisdom and knowledge, that I may lead these people, for who is able to govern these people of yours?'"

Solomon made a wise choice and his request pleased God. Look at Second Chronicles 1:11-12: "God said to Solomon, since this is your heart's desire and you have not asked for wealth, riches or honor, nor for the death of your enemy, and since you have not asked for a long life but for wisdom and knowledge to govern my people over whom I have made you king. Therefore, wisdom and knowledge will be given you. And I will also give you wealth, riches, and honor." How did Solomon know how to respond to God's question? Did he just get lucky and just happen to think about asking God for wisdom? Not a chance.

Solomon writes in Proverbs 4:3-7: "When I was a boy in my father's house, still tender, and an only child of my mother, he taught me and said, 'Lay hold of my words with all your heart; keep my commands and you will live. Get wisdom, get understanding; Do not forget my words or swerve from them. Do not forsake wisdom; and she will protect you.'"

David invested in Solomon. He took time to share his life lessons with Solomon, and he gave him wisdom about life. David took time with his son and helped him to learn the ways of God. What an investment.

Challenge for today: Answer these questions: Who are you investing in? To whom are you teaching the ways of God? The greatest investment you will ever make is not in a blue-chip stock. But the greatest investment you will ever make is in the life of someone that God has put in front of you. Take time to open your eyes to see who that is. Teach them the things that God has shown you. Give them encouragement and hold them accountable. You will find great joy. Invest in others and it will come back tenfold.

Not Qualified? Guess Again.

In First Samuel 16:1 the Lord said to Samuel: "I am sending you to Jesse of Bethlehem. I have chosen one of his sons to be king."

So, Samuel left for Bethlehem to anoint a king. First Samuel 16:6: "When they arrived, Samuel saw Eliab and thought, Surely the Lord's anointing stands here before the Lord."

It would have made sense because he was a big, strong, good looking, young man, and he was the eldest son. But God did not choose him. As a matter of fact, seven sons of Jesse passed before Samuel, and God did not choose them as king. In First Samuel 16:11 Samuel said to Jesse: "Are these all your sons you have?" Jesse said, 'There is still the youngest, but he is tending the sheep.' Samuel said, 'Send for him: we will not sit down until he arrives.'"

When David arrived back at home, the Lord told Samuel to rise and anoint him as king. Who would have picked David as king? Was he even qualified? He wasn't even invited to the king's anointing party.

That was not the only time David would be overlooked. How about the story of David and Goliath? Was David qualified to fight a giant or did the people really believe he could defeat the Philistine champion? No. In First Samuel 17:28, David's oldest brother heard David scheme to fight the giant, and he was mad. He asked David, "Why have you come down here and whom did you leave the sheep with?"

David was so little he couldn't even wear the armor. What could this little boy do with the nine-foot killing machine? I am sure he heard the criticism and the people's unbelief. But David followed through with what God called him to do. He wasn't Saul's top choice to fight Goliath, and he wasn't qualified by the world's standards. He was God's choice.

First Samuel 16:7: Samuel said, "The Lord doesn't look at the things man looks at. Man looks at the outward appearance, but the Lord looks at the heart."

The world may tell you that you are not qualified or that you are not ready. They may even put you down and criticize what God has put in your heart. But if God is for you, who can be against you?

Challenge for today: Follow your dreams and your passion that God has put inside of you. Don't listen to the crowds and the critics that come your way. Set your eyes on the Father and follow hard after Him. I love Acts 4:13, when Peter and John stood in front of the religious, high-class leaders of Jesus's day. It says: "When they saw the courage of Peter and John and realized they were unschooled, ordinary men, they were astonished, and they took note that these men had been with Jesus."

Not qualified? Guess again.

The I Bomb

Satan embodies the character of self. Look at Isaiah's quote of Lucifer: Isaiah 14:13-14: "You said in your heart, 'I will ascend into heaven; I will raise my throne above the stars of God; I will sit enthroned on the mount of assembly, on the utmost heights of the sacred mountain. I will ascend above the tops of the clouds; I will make myself like the Most High.'"

Satan was full of himself. Romans 8:8 says, "Those controlled by the sinful nature cannot please God."

Self will do anything before it dies. It will pray, teach Sunday School, and tithe. It will even preach. It will steep itself in religious traditions to cushion itself against God. Selfishness is an enemy of God. Christ didn't come to improve 'self', but to replace it. It's not a changed life, but an exchanged life. There is but one cure for self...DEATH. Galatians 2:20: "I have been crucified with Christ and I no longer live, but Christ lives in me."

We are crucified in Christ, and the cross has set us free. We are risen with Christ, and He lives and reigns in us. If you are anything like me, selfishness and pride are continuous struggles. We want to have control of every situation and the people around us. We want to be comfortable, and we want to have the reins in our hands. Don't forget what God has told us. Those controlled by the sinful nature cannot please God. Here is my question: Does your life please God?

Challenge for today: Surrender fully to Christ and ask Him to take His rightful place. Let go of the reins of your heart and give Him total control. Humble yourself before Jesus' feet today and surrender it all to His Lordship. Make a list of the things that you are holding back from the Lord. Set aside time to talk with your Heavenly Father about it.

There Is More

Matthew 11:28: "Come to me, all you who are weary and burdened, and I will give you rest." There is immediate rest to the one who responds to the Savior's invitation. Just to walk into the arms of God is like none other. What a blessing to become a child of God and enjoy the rest of forgiveness. But there is more. Matthew 11:29-30: "Take my yoke upon you and learn from me, for I am gentle and humble in heart, and you will find rest for your soul. For my yoke is easy and my burden is light."

This is the rest of the soul. The rest of forgiveness depends on coming to Jesus and the rest of the soul depends on taking the yoke of Jesus. The yoke is the symbol of submission. This is fully submitting to the will of God and trusting Him with everything. We can study the Bible from cover to cover and spend hours and hours digging, but one hour in the yoke of Christ will teach you more than all of this. Submission is the secret to learning and rest. This means we must accept the authority of His Lordship and acknowledge Him as Lord of our life. Get into the harness with Christ. When we are fully submitted to Christ, we can trust Him with all the little details. There are so many things we try to control and manipulate. We spend hours and even days worrying about things that may not even happen. We begin to play the what if game. Do you have the rest of forgiveness? Do you have rest for your soul? Jump in the harness of Christ and live in a whole new world of peace.

Challenge for today: Jesus said, "Come to me." He is offering invitations to a whole new way of living. Surrender the controls and stop trying to manipulate situations and people for your benefit. He is calling you to surrender. He is calling you to service. He is calling you to his harness to join Him in a mission of a lifetime. Yoke up, Church.

Immeasurably More

Ephesians 3:20: "Now to him who is able to do immeasurably more than all we ask or imagine, according to his power that is at work in us."

What dreams has God put in your heart? What is that immeasurably more, for your life?

Many of us as Jesus followers miss our destiny on earth because we are so focused on ourselves. We focus on ourselves because we underestimate and don't trust God. We are guilty of not praying like we should. Prayer is the weapon that unleashes the power of God and brings dying people to the foot of the cross. If you are in Christ, He has placed eternity in your heart. You have an appetite from God that you will never lose, that which will last forever. Anything else is just too small. A life that is filled with mostly earthly stuff and earthly pursuits is going to leave you unsatisfied. God has made you restless for more because He wants to eternalize your life-to make it count for something that will last forever.

The passion to make a greater difference with the rest of your life is from the One who gave you life. God takes you from your small, small world to a life bigger than you could ever dream. Here I am Lord, use me. You can't shrink back in fear and stop dreaming those God dreams. The Lord is inviting you to join Him on His mission to do immeasurably more and to reach this world for Jesus Christ. God bless. Dare to dream.

Challenge for today: Spend extra time in prayer and really take a long look at your life? Don't be scared to ask yourself questions about your passions and dreams. Are there passions in your life that God has given you, that you have dropped or left behind because of fear or discouragement? Do you seem to be stuck in life and are you just existing? Tell God that you are tired of just existing. Ask Him to shine His light on your old dreams and place a fire in your heart for new passions. Dare to dream big dreams because we serve a huge God.

You Can Trust Him

In John 19:10-11 "Pilate asked Jesus, 'Don't you realize I have power either to free you, or to crucify You?' Then Jesus answered him, 'You would have no power over Me, unless it has been given to you from above.'"

Jesus also spoke in Matthew 10:29, "Are not two sparrows sold for a penny? Yet not one of them will fall to the ground apart from the will of your Father."

Whether the circumstance is big or small, we must know God is in control.

Psalm 103:19: "The Lord has established his throne in the heavens, and his kingdom rules over all."

I don't know why bad things happen to good people. There are a lot of things that happen on this side of eternity that make me stop and scratch my head. Many circumstances are not God's perfect will, but He allows them through His permissive will. Through it all, we need to trust Him. Our lives belong to our sovereign, all knowing, and loving God. I hate to say this, but it is the truth. I hate the difficulty or the test while I am in it, and I wonder why I had to face it. But on the other side, I can see why He allowed it. Romans 8:28 promises: "And we know that in all things God works for the good of those who love him, who have been called according to his purpose."

What a promise we have in Jesus Christ. Hang on to this truth as you walk your faith out in this crazy world. Put your faith into the hands of someone you can trust, Jesus.

Challenge for today: During those tough times, remind yourself that God has your best interests in his heart. There is no reason to doubt Him because His love is perfect. Trusting Him means to look beyond what we can see. Know that He sees the entire picture from the beginning to the end. He is your loving Father that wants the best for your life.

Eternal Security

Does it really matter if we believe in eternal security? You better believe it. Eternity is one of God's promises, and He wants us to be confident about our future with Him. First John 5:13: "I write these things to you who believe in the name of the Son of God so that you may know that you have eternal life."

A believer who is sure of eternity is not working to get something from God but is serving Him out of pure devotion. Ephesians 2:8-9: "For it is by grace you have been saved, through faith-and this is not from yourselves, it is a gift of God-not of works, so that no one could boast."

Grace is a gift. If we add a single work requirement to salvation, then it is no longer a gift. If salvation is based on anything other than the completed work of Jesus Christ on the cross, then we find ourselves on unstable ground. John 10:27-30: "My sheep listen to my voice; I know them, and they follow me. I give them eternal life, and they shall never perish; no one can snatch them out of my hand. My Father, who has given them to me, is greater than all, no one can snatch them out of my Father's hand. I and the Father are one."

Hang on to this truth. If you are in Christ, you are eternally secure in the Lord. When we received Jesus as our Savior, we didn't receive just forgiveness, we received life. Through the Holy Spirit, Jesus is right now abiding in us. He has promised that He would not leave us, nor forsake us, but He has sent us a helper.

John 14:6: "Jesus answered, I am the way and the truth and the life. No one comes to the Father except through me." Do you have a love relationship with the Father? Jesus is the only way to secure your eternal security and the only way to know true peace. You cannot find it any other way. Are you prepared to face eternity? Turn your eyes upon Jesus. God bless and have a great day.

Challenge for today: Thank God for the gift of grace. Thank Him for the gift of salvation and eternal life. Thank Him for His never-ending love and the promises of His Word. He has provided a way of salvation and has given us a promise of eternal security. Praise Him today.

Waiting On God

Waiting is probably one of the most difficult things that Christians are asked to do. This is especially true when there is something that seems to be right at your fingertips, and we feel this is God's will for our lives. But God has a clear plan for telling us to wait. Waiting is a huge part of learning how-to walk-in obedience to God. Being patient is difficult but failing to wait on God can be much worse.

1. When we don't wait on God, we get out of God's will.
2. We delay God's planned blessings for us because we moved ahead of Him.
3. We are prone to make rash decisions that may cost us down the road.

How many times have we taken our eyes off Christ and tried to manipulate our situation to conform to our will? Whenever we reach for something that is not of God, it will fall to pieces. Wait on the Lord. I want to share a couple of scriptures that God has placed on my heart.

Psalm 27:14: "Wait for the Lord; be strong and let your heart take courage; yes, wait for the Lord."

Psalm 37:4-7: "Delight yourself in the Lord; and He will give you the desires of your heart. Commit your way to the Lord, trust also in Him, and He will do it. He will bring forth your righteousness as the light and your judgment as the noonday. Rest in the Lord and wait patiently for Him."

Isaiah 40:31: "Yet those who wait in the Lord will renew their strength. They will soar on wings like eagles; they will run and not grow weary, they will walk and not faint."

Remember, waiting and trusting are inseparable. Wait on God's green light and the peace that comes when it is time to move. Believe me, I know it is hard to wait on the Lord. Just know that God has heard your prayers, and He is working behind the scenes. He wants what is best for you. Trust and obey.

Challenge for today: When there are decisions to be made, whether they are small or big, wait on God's green light. In everything you do, make sure you cover it all in prayer. Wait on the Lord, be strong in your faith, and trust Him to lead you with love. Don't grow impatient and get ahead of God. Wait and let God go before you and prepare the way. I am sure God's way will turn out a lot better than your way.

Blessed?

I am sitting here in my kitchen feeling extremely blessed. I am blessed because of my health, my family, good friends, and my faith in Jesus Christ. How about you? There is a verse that has jumped off the page at me, that I want to share with you. Romans 4:7-8 says, "Blessed are they whose transgressions are forgiven, whose sins are covered. Blessed is the man whose sins the Lord will never count against him."

We all mess up and some mess up more than others. There are things in my life that I am not proud of and wish I could go back and get a do over. But thank God for the truth we find in Romans 3:21-24: "But now a righteousness from God, apart from the law, has been made known, to which the Law and the Prophets testify. This righteousness from God comes through faith in Jesus Christ to all who believe. There is no difference, for all have sinned and fall short of the glory of God and are justified freely by His grace and the redemption that came by Jesus Christ."

In Christ, because of His ultimate sacrifice and God's amazing grace, we can experience forgiveness. We are made right in the sight of God and set free from the grips of sin and bondage for all those who receive His gift. Check out this Good News in Romans 10:9-13, "That if you confess with your mouth, 'Jesus is Lord,' and believe in your heart that God raised him from the dead, you will be saved. For it is with your heart that you believe and are justified, and it is with your mouth that you confess and are saved. As the scripture says, 'Anyone who trusts in him will never be put to shame.' There is no difference between Jew and Gentile-the same Lord is Lord of all and richly blesses all who call on him, for, 'Everyone who calls on the name of the Lord will be saved.'"

Have you experienced His forgiveness? Have you trusted Him as your Lord and Savior? Have you been set free from shame, guilt, and regret? Are you blessed?

I want to close with First John 1:8-9: "If we claim to be without sin, we deceive ourselves and the truth is not in us. If we confess our sins, he is faithful and just and will forgive us our sins and purify us from all unrighteousness."

Challenge for today: Dump it all at the Lord's feet. Blessed are those whose sins are forgiven. What are you waiting for? Are you tired of carrying your bag of regrets and sins around? In time, that will wear you down. Go to the Lord and confess your sins; lay it all at His feet. Receive His mercy and grace. Then count your blessings, and name them one by one. Experience the wonderful gift of grace.

Break Out the Harp

Have you ever been in that rut in life when you know something is missing? Or it seems like you just can't catch a break. You are wanting a breakthrough or something just to happen to break up the same ole, same ole. It's that time in life when everything you touch seems to fall apart and you are tired and worn out. Then break out the harp.

Psalm 33:1-4: "Sing joyful to the Lord, you righteous; it is fitting for the upright to praise him. Praise the Lord with the harp; make music to him on the ten-string lyre. Sing to him a new song; play skillfully, and shout for joy. For the word of the Lord is right and true; he is faithful in all he does."

I encourage you to worship. When the craziness of life has you down, or when you feel overwhelmed and beat up, worship. You may say, "I can't play a harp or a lyre, but I can sure pop on Pandora, and I can shout." We were created to worship. Something happens when we worship, and we finally take our eyes off ourselves. When you take time to worship, don't hold back. Rock it out, shout, or even dance before the Lord. He is worthy of our praise.

Psalm 98:4-9: "Shout for joy to the Lord, all the earth. Burst into jubilant song with music; make music to the Lord with the harp, with the harp and the sound of singing, with trumpets and the blast of the ram's horn-shout for joy before the Lord, the King. Let the rivers clap their hands, let the mountains sing together for joy; let them sing before the Lord, for he comes to judge the earth. He will judge the world in righteousness and the peoples with equity."

Challenge for today: Ask the Father to take over. Ask Him to help you be positive and encouraging. Ask Him to help you take your eyes off yourself and turn your focus to Him. Break out "The Harp" and worship because He is faithful in all He does. Worship, worship, and worship some more! Amen.

Intimacy With God

There is no substitute for personal intimacy with the Lord. Think about this: Most of us are looking for an exciting and fulfilling life, but we are looking in all the wrong places: money, power, and relationships. We are looking for something that can bring us fulfillment and personal joy. There is a God-shaped void in all of us. The only thing that can fill that void is God's presence. The gift of His Son abiding in us is more than adequate for everything we do. He is enough.

It's great to have goals, dreams, and great relationships, but our primary pursuit should be to know God. God is calling us to an intimate relationship with Him. Pursue His presence! Psalms 27:1-8: "The Lord is my light and my salvation-whom shall I fear? The Lord is the stronghold of my life-of whom shall I be afraid? When evil men advance against me to devour my flesh, when my enemies and my foes attack me, they stumble and fall, though an army besiege me, my heart will not fear; though war break out against me, even then will I be confident. One thing I ask of the Lord, this is what I seek; that I may dwell in the house of the Lord all the days of my life, to gaze upon the beauty of the Lord and seek him in his temple. For in the day of trouble he will keep me safe in his dwelling; he will hide me in the shelter of his tabernacle and set me high upon a rock. Then my head will be exalted above the enemies who surround me; at his tabernacle will I sacrifice with shouts of joy; I will sing and make music to the Lord. Hear my voice when I call, O Lord, be merciful to me and answer me. My heart says of you, 'Seek his face!' Your face, Lord, I will seek."

What are you pursuing and running after? What has first place in your life and how do you spend most of your available time? What dreams are you chasing?

Challenge for today: I want to encourage you to set aside time every single day to soak in the presence of God. That's right, I said, "soak." This means to sit in the presence of God and wait there until you hear His voice. Don't get in a hurry but enjoy resting in your Father's arms. It means talking with your Savior and giving Him time to talk back. It will change your life. Don't forget this fact, we were created to worship Him. Thank the Lord for the privilege. We must soak in His presence.

Eat Up

I want to give you some scripture that we all need from time to time. Temptation will come when we least expect it, and I don't care who you are or how strong you claim to be. Scripture will help you to remain strong. Psalm 119:9-12: "How can a young man keep his way pure? By living according to your word. I seek you with all my heart; don't let me stray from your commands. I have hidden your word in my heart that I might not sin against you."

Satan is good at what he does, and he is very determined to destroy your life. Don't forget that he hates you, and he will do anything to discourage you and to lead you down the wrong path. He knows his destination, but he wants to drag as many people to hell with him as he can. If he can't, he wants to make your life as miserable as possible.

I encourage you to feed your spirit every day by diving into God's Word. Eat up. It will give you the spiritual nutrition you need to grow and to develop. Who in their right mind would send out an army to fight who has not eaten in a week? Feed your spirit and starve the flesh. It is time to pull up to the buffet of Heaven and dine with the King. Growing up I was always short and skinny. I didn't have time to stop and eat. As soon as I ate a few bites, I was ready to race off and return to what I was doing. My mom always told me, "You have to start eating more if you are going to grow up to be strong and tall." Church, we need to start eating more if we are going to grow up to be strong and tall. Let the Word fill you with truth and wisdom. Hold on to the teachings of Jesus Christ. The Word of God will change your life forever. Eat up, Church.

Challenge for today: Make it a priority in your life to open the Word of God. Change your mindset. It is not that we "got to", but we "get to". What a privilege it is to be able to have a copy of God's Word, the anointed words of God. The more you dig, the more you will find. I want to challenge you to increase your personal study time and make sure you share this commitment with someone close to you. We all need some accountability. Let God's Word go deep.

Some Things Never Change

Some things never change. Atlanta traffic is one of those things. Don't you hate when you are driving through downtown Atlanta, and everything seems fine. Traffic is flowing, and then you see the brake lights. It is not a good situation, and it may cost a lot of time waiting in traffic. Not only does Atlanta traffic never change, but there is also something else that never changes. Hebrews 13:8 tells us, "Jesus Christ is the same yesterday and today and forever."

Can I get an Amen? That is something we can take to the bank and that is someone we can trust in. He has, and will, and always will be the King of kings and the Lord of lords. He is the Forever God. Jeremiah 33:11: "Give thanks to the Lord Almighty, for the Lord is good: his love endures forever."

His love never changes no matter what we do or how many times we fall. His love endures forever, and it never changes.

Psalm 146:6: "The maker of heaven and earth, the sea, and everything in them-the Lord, who remains faithful forever."

Our forever faithful God will never leave us or forsake us. That is a promise straight from the Word of God. That is something we can stand on and hold to when the storms of life come.

Isaiah 40:8: "The grass withers and the flowers fall, but the word of our God stands forever."

The things of this world will one day pass away. Money, fancy trucks, and lavish homes will one day crumble, but God's Word will last forever. It never changes. It will stand the test of time because it is Truth. "Yes, Lord." The Lord reigns forever. My salvation is found in the blood of Jesus Christ, and one day I will spend eternity with my Savior. That is something I can hold on to and never let go of. That will never change. He is the same yesterday, today, and forever.

Isaiah 40:28: "Do you not know? Have you not heard? The Lord is the everlasting God, the Creator of the ends of the earth. He will not grow tired or weary, and his understanding no one can fathom."

He never changes. He never stops loving, and He never stops being faithful. He is trustworthy and you can lean on Him in any situation. "Thank you, Lord, for who you are. You are my rock. You are my high tower. You are my forever God."

Challenge for today: List three things that you are grateful for that God has blessed you with. Take time to praise the everlasting Father who cares for you day in and day out. List two ways God has shown you, His faithfulness. I hope you have a great day.

Bringing Glory to Your Father

Today God has given us another day, and He has given us another opportunity to bring Him glory. In John 17:4: "Jesus said, I brought glory to you here on earth by doing everything you told me to do."

Jesus honored God but fulfilled his purpose on earth. What is your purpose? Are you being obedient to the calling in your life? Is your life bringing God glory? I want to share with you five ways you can bring God glory by fulfilling your purpose.

1. We bring glory to God by worshiping Him.

Romans 6:13: "Do not offer the parts of your body to sin, as instruments of wickedness, but rather offer yourself to God, as those who have been brought from death to life; and offer the parts of your body to him as instruments of righteousness." Worship is a lifestyle of enjoying God and giving ourselves to His purpose.

2. We bring glory to God by loving others.

Romans 15:7: "Accept each other just as Christ has accepted you; then God will be glorified." We need to love others how Christ loved us. Lord, give me that kind of love.

3. We bring glory to God by becoming more like Christ.

Second Corinthians 3:18: "As the Spirit of the Lord works within us, we become more and more like Him and reflect His glory even more." Christ is calling us to growth. He is calling us into maturity.

4. We bring glory to God when we use our gifts.

First Peter 4:10: "Each one should use whatever gift he has received to serve others." God has given each believer a gift and we are called to use it to glorify Him. Put it into use to encourage others. It will bring you peace, fulfillment, and joy, but it will also bring God glory.

5. We bring God glory by telling others about Jesus Christ.

We have a message that can change the world. God's desire is for His church to share the Good News that Jesus is alive and well. This is our privilege.

John 12:27-28: "Now my heart is troubled, and what shall I say? Father, save me from this hour? No, it was for this very reason I came to this hour. Father, glorify your name!"

I have read this before, but it has never grabbed my attention like this. Jesus stood at a fork in the road. Would He fulfill His purpose and bring glory to His Father? We all know that Jesus didn't shrink back or live for his own self-centered purpose. He willingly died for the sake of mankind to fulfill His purpose. Are we living for our own goals and our own pleasures? Are we living life for His glory? It all comes down to one question. Who are you going to live for? You or God? Real life begins by fully committing yourself completely to Jesus Christ.

Romans 11:36: "For everything comes from God alone. Everything lives by His power, and everything is for His glory."

Challenge for today: Living for God's glory is a decision you will have to make. Yes, it may mean changing your priorities, your schedule, the way you spend money, and your friendships. Does it sometimes mean choosing a difficult path? Yes, but there is nothing like fulfilling your purpose in life and being totally content. Take time to evaluate your life and ask God if your life is pleasing to Him. I know it's a tough question to ask God. Go ahead, I dare you.

This Verse Again?

Jeremiah 29:11: "For I know the plans I have for you," declares the Lord," plans to prosper you and not to harm you, plans to give you hope and a future."

We all know sooner or later; troubles will come our way. We will all face hard times, and most of the time we can learn, grow, and become what God has called us to be. Having troubles doesn't automatically produce what God intends.

Sometimes we become bitter rather than better. We have learned to respond to hard times the way Jesus would. We must remember that God's plan is good, but God's ways are not always our ways. I think we all could agree with that. God does know what is best. It is vital that we stay focused on God's plan, not on the pain or the situation at hand.

Hebrews 12:2: "Let us fix our eyes on Jesus, the author and perfecter of our faith."

Corrie ten Boom said, "If you look at the world, you will be distressed. If you look within, you'll be depressed. But if you look to Christ you'll be at rest." Keep your eyes on Christ. Pain is temporary, but your reward will be eternal. Don't give in to short-term thinking. I want to encourage you with three things if you are facing difficult times.

1. Stay positive and thankful.

Spend extra time in prayer. God's Word tells us to be thankful in all things. God is at work in your life, and He has a plan and a purpose for you. Hang on to that promise. I know it is hard to wait. But while you wait, stay positive.

2. Fight and don't give up.

Character building is a slow process. Whenever we try to avoid or escape the problems of life, we can short circuit the process, and delay our growth. Don't give up but grow up.

3. Use your talent.

Use your gift that God has blessed you with when you are overwhelmed with situations, grief, and troubles.

Challenge for today: Don't sit back and feel sorry for yourself or pull a blanket over your head. Kick the devil in the teeth and use your gifts for the Glory of God. It will do wonders for your soul.

Get It Right

In Matthew 22:37-39: "Jesus said, 'Love the Lord your God with all your heart and with all your soul and with all your mind.' This is the first and greatest and foremost commandment. And the second is like it, 'You shall love your neighbor as yourself.'"

God places extreme importance on relationships. He is more interested in us having the right relationship than He is receiving an offering. Matthew 5:23-24: "Therefore if you are presenting your offering at the altar, and there remember that your brother has something against you, leave your offering there before the altar and go; first be reconciled to your brother, and then come and present your offering."

How hard is that? I don't know about you, but I don't like confrontation. I would prefer to ignore the negative situation and work my way around it. We all have those people who we try to ignore. Don't lie - you know you do. Have you ever been in the store, and you see that one person that you just don't like? There is something about them that just hits you the wrong way. So, you act like you don't see them, and you dodge them by heading down the next aisle. Here is the verse God put in front of me today. First John 4:20: "If someone says, 'I love God,' and hates his brother, he is a liar; for one who does not love his brother whom he has seen, cannot love God whom he has not seen."

Talking about getting your toes stepped on. Let's get real. Who did God just put in front of you? You have been ignoring these people for years. You have been dodging them every time you see them. There are hurt feelings and pain, but God is saying to make things right.

Challenge for today: Stop walking in sin and disobedience. It's time to swallow your pride and do what God has asked you to do. I didn't say it was going to be easy. And yes, God did put someone in front of me today. Listen and obey. He blesses obedience. Stop making excuses and get it right.

Willing To Be Real

God loves to use weak people. Think about it, we all have weaknesses. Usually, I try to deny it and even try to cover them up. It's amazing how God changes our thinking the older we get. I have always thought that God only wanted to use our strengths, but He wants to use our weaknesses too. First Corinthians 1:27: "But God chose the foolish things of the world to shame the wise; God chose the weak things of the world to shame the strong."

Your weaknesses are not an accident. God uses your weaknesses in your life to demonstrate His power through you. God loves taking ordinary people, despite their flaws, to do extraordinary things. If God only used perfect people, nothing would ever get done. If you want to be used by God, you must first be willing to admit your weaknesses. Stop pretending you have it all together. Drop the sideshow, and let people see who you really are. Real ministry begins with vulnerability. We must learn to take off our masks and be willing to share our own struggles. At some point in our lives, we must decide if we want to impress people or influence people. People will begin to trust you not by being perfect, but by being honest.

Jesus spoke in Second Corinthians 12:9: "My grace is sufficient for you, for my power is made perfect in weakness."

I love to write, but I am not a good writer. Writing my thoughts down has always been one of my biggest weaknesses. When I surrendered my entire life to the Lord, I was saying to Him no matter what you call be to do, my answer is yes. Why am I not surprised He asked me to write a devotional book? He loves to be glorified in our weakness. To You be the glory.

Challenge for today: Are we limiting God's power in our lives by trying to hide our weaknesses? Stop the pretense and get real with God and others. That is where real ministry begins. I hope you have a great day.

A Simple Thought

God is good, and He is good all the time. I want to look at a verse that made me stop and think. Acts 13:36: "David served God's purpose in his generation."

We all know that David wasn't perfect. Just like most of us, he stumbled and fell a couple of times. But David dedicated his life to fulfilling God's purpose on earth. My prayer is that people will be able to say that about me after I die, and I also pray the same for you.

Second Chronicles 16:9: "For the eyes of the Lord range throughout the earth to strengthen those who are fully committed to Him."

God is looking for those who want to make a difference. He is calling out to those who are fully committed to sharing the Good News of Jesus Christ. He is searching for those who will love others unconditionally and serve Him faithfully. I want to give you something to think about today. Take time to ask yourself some questions throughout the day. Will you be that person that God can use for His purpose? Are you willing to say yes to God's plan for your life? What is your purpose for living? What has God gifted you to do? Are you even using that gift? Do you honestly feel like you are at the center of God's will for your life? Are you content? Are you at peace with how you are living out your life? Those are some heavy questions, but they need to be answered. Say yes to Jesus. Say yes to His calling.

Challenge for today: Be willing to use your gifts and passions for the glory of God. I urge you to live life without regret. Serve the Lord with gladness and live a life that will make God smile.

Do You Worry or Worship?

What is most important to you? We can center our lives around our career, family, sports, or a hobby. These things are all good, but they don't belong at the center of your life. Whatever is at the center of your life is your god. So how can you know when God is at the center of your life? When God is at the center, you will worship. When he's not, you will worry. Are you spending more time worrying than you are worshiping? If so, you need to put Him back in the center of your life.

Philippians 4:6-7 says, "Do not be anxious about anything, but in everything, by prayer and petition, with thanksgiving, present your request to God. And the peace of God, which transcends all understanding, will guard your hearts and minds in Christ Jesus."

I want to encourage you to spend more time in prayer. Start a prayer journal and watch how your prayer life can come alive. When you are communicating with God, you can't help but worship Him. Put God back where He belongs, at the center of your life. Let Him have His way with you. Let go of worry and stress. Trust God with all your heart and rest in Him.

Proverbs 3:5-6 tells us this, "Trust in the Lord with all your heart and lean not on your own understanding; in all your ways acknowledge him, and he will make your paths straight."

Place your worries in the hands of the very Creator of heaven and earth and worship Him with all your heart.

Challenge for today: Memorize Proverbs 3:5-6 and let it serve as a reminder of who we need to trust. Take a hard look at your life and ask yourself this question. Is Christ sitting on the throne of my heart? Do I put more trust in myself and my abilities than I do my heavenly Father? Worship Him, seek His presence, and trust Him with your life...even the so-called 'little stuff.'

The Keys to Staying on Track

Luke 2:52: "Jesus grew in wisdom and stature, and favor with God and men." Hear me today, Jesus is the total package. He had balance in his life. Just like Jesus, we need balance in our lives. I want to give you four things that will help you to have continual spiritual growth in your life.

1. Have a spiritual mentor and be involved in a small group.

Proverbs 27:17 says, "As iron sharpens iron, so one man sharpens another."

We need community, and we need encouragement. Who is challenging you to grow in your walk with Jesus? We all need a mentor.

2. Give yourself regular spiritual checkups.

God's Word says in Lamentations 3:40: "Let us examine our ways and test them and let us return to the Lord."

Sometimes we must reset. Ask yourself some serious questions about your spiritual growth and your relationship with Jesus Christ. Set aside time every couple of months to check your spiritual health.

3. Write down your progress in a war journal.

Record what God is doing in your life. Even write down the hard life lessons you had to learn along the way.

Hebrews 2:11 says, "We must pay careful attention, therefore, to what we have heard, so that we don't drift away."

Write down your doubts, fears, victories, and defeats. God will use all of this to mold you and shape you. Plus, it is always good to go back and see just how faithful God is.

4. Pass on what God has shown you to others. If you want to grow, teach others what God has shown you.

Proverbs 11:25 says, "A generous man will prosper; he who refreshes others will himself be refreshed."

God has called each of us to be His messengers. We are to share the truth of God's Word and to tell the world that Jesus is alive and well. Invest in others. Blessed are the balanced.

Challenge for today: Apply these four steps to your life. Spend some time praying over each one and ask God to help you stay on track in your walk with Him. These four steps may seem so insignificant, but the neglect of these four disciplines is a huge reason why so many people stumble and fall in their relationship with Jesus Christ. Stay on track and continue to grow in your walk with Christ. God has placed certain people in your life for a reason.

About The Author

I started in Student Ministry when I was twenty years old, and it was my calling for nearly thirty years. My heart was for students to come to know Christ, and to grow in their relationship with Him. I love to see God's light bulb fill their eyes and hearts, and I loved sharing the Gospel of Jesus with students who everybody else said was a lost cause. My passion was not only to teach them about a relationship with the Lord, but it was also to give them a real-life example of what it looked like to be walked out in everyday life. My time alone with God has always been my rock, my fortress, and my high tower. Spending time each morning in prayer, reading God's Word, and taking time to listen to His voice has changed my life forever. I love sharing with young believers who dare to dive deep into the river of God's love. It is so rewarding to invest in the life of other people, watching them go from the shallow end of faith and dive into the deep water of a love relationship with Jesus.

I had the privilege of pastoring two churches, and they both were a huge blessing to me and my family. The Lord led us to plant a church in Leesburg, Georgia. It was a time of growth, and a time of great joy. I loved preaching God's Word on a weekly basis, encouraging, and loving on families. We started with twelve people in our home one Sunday morning, a short time later God opened the door to purchase a building on a couple of acres in Lee County. That church is still going strong and is known as Forrester Community Church. I also had the honor to pastor Salem Baptist Church in Worth County, Georgia. Salem is a small country church with a huge heart for God and their community. I was there for a short time, but they have a very special place in my heart.

Today, I serve as the Pastor of Sports and Recreation at Park Avenue in Titusville, Florida. Peter Lord was the founding pastor of Park Avenue Baptist Church. He was also the author of several well-known books such as Hearing God, Soul Care, 959 plan, and many more. He was one of the greatest communicators of God's Word that I have ever heard in person. I had the honor of being discipled by this great man of God back in 2004, as I served as the Senior High Student Pastor. My role today at Park Avenue is to use sports and recreation to reach out to the community around us. As we develop relationships through sports, God provides us an open door to share our Jesus with them and their families. My hope, my joy, and my calling is to lead as many people as possible into a saving relationship with Jesus. Then encourage them to take those next steps to grow and mature in their faith

Made in the USA
Columbia, SC
11 April 2022

58791963R00115